Sue Miller gained a BSc (Hons) in Psychology as a mature student in 1992, followed by a professional qualification in social work (DipSW) in 1995 and a Postgraduate Diploma in Social Work in 1996. Sue is registered to practice as a child-care social worker and works in a statutory setting within the Department of Health and Social Care of the Local Authority.

Aged 54, Sue continues to live in the small village of her childhood in the North-West of England with husband, Martin. Sue has two sisters, three children and four grandchildren; all live locally.

DEATH OF A SOCIAL WORKER

Sue Miller

Death of a Social Worker

Vanguard Press

VANGUARD PAPERBACK

© Copyright 2008
Sue Miller

A CIP catalogue record for this title is
available from the British Library.

ISBN 978 184386 466 0

*Vanguard Press is an imprint of
Pegasus Elliot MacKenzie Publishers Ltd.*
www.pegasuspublishers.com

First Published in 2008

**Vanguard Press
Sheraton House Castle Park
Cambridge England**

Printed & Bound in Great Britain

Dedication

"It is dangerous to be right when those in power are wrong".

Voltaire

This book is dedicated to all who seek to make a difference, whether in their own lives, that of others, or both. Good luck and my heartfelt best wishes in your endeavours.

It is also dedicated to the memory of Margaret, Robert and Paul, who will remain in my heart forever.

Acknowledgements

The list of people I would like to thank for making the writing of this book possible is endless; everyone I have ever known, in both a personal and professional capacity, has taught me much – one way or another.

My family is my life and I would like to thank each and every member for supporting me, just by 'being' my family. I would also like to thank colleagues, past and present, for putting up with me and my 'soapbox', in my endeavours to make sense of it all.

Finally, I would like to point out that I have tried to disguise identifying features, including names, specific geographical areas, my employers, service users and myself – for obvious reasons. Of course, those who know me well and those about whom I have written in detail will almost certainly recognise themselves and me. I hope I have represented us fairly and without malice.

PROLOGUE

I was born to be a social worker, or so I had always thought. Now this may have been naïve, and of course I needed to earn a living to support my three children and myself, but my beliefs and values have always been important to me. My work had to be meaningful as opposed to just being a job. Social work to me was a vocation as well as a career and I felt I had much to offer; I still do.

We all damage our children, as we ourselves have been damaged by our parents; it's just a matter of degree. I've never known anyone who isn't carrying baggage, including myself, but the extent to which it impacts upon us and our children is mediated by a number of other variables. Most 'damage' is unintentional and occurs as a result of lack of knowledge and self-analysis and/or the situations, circumstances and life events we are exposed to, in addition to our capacity to cope and the support networks available to us. The 'good' social worker is insightful, has life experience and has the skills necessary to help families identify and work through their difficulties, where appropriate, and only as a last resort separates children from their families, on the basis of what is best for the child. This is the theory.

In reality, social workers tend to attract bad press, being variously portrayed as do-gooders, incompetent, interfering or uncaring; often a combination of all these things. A great deal of time, money and effort is poured into pre- and post-qualification training and re-training of social workers, in an effort to evidence continuous improvement and to appease critics, and in response to the latest report of an inquiry or research findings and changes in legislation, policies and procedures. Of course, it is an impossible task and those that fare worst are Local Authority, front-line, childcare workers who are increasingly held responsible and accountable for situations and outcomes far beyond their control.

How it works is that the more experienced, knowledgeable, skilled and 'caring' a worker is, the more de-skilled, frustrated and overloaded they become. Those of us who have played the 'social work game' know exactly what this means but have little opportunity to redress the balance. I'm not talking perfection here, just the difference between holding your head above water and being able to exercise professional judgement, based on academic and experiential knowledge, or being closed down, engaging in bad practice and protecting yourself.

I have never set out to be radical in my practice or beliefs and I understand the constraints within which we have to work. My concern is whether or not this makes it right; a simple enough question, and one which most practitioners and social work managers do not have the time, energy or inclination to consider. It is not my intention to point the finger of blame towards any individual or group of individuals; after all, we chose our careers because we wanted to make a difference, didn't we? And nothing I have to say will be a revelation to anyone 'in the business', who has taken the time to consider their own place in the order of things.

Local authority social work is in crisis; in fact its condition is terminal. What follows is a very personal account of my own journey through the minefield of life in general and social work in particular. I struggled to find a format for my writing, eventually settling on an autobiographical, personal approach rather than an academic one. In this way I hope to illustrate the interface between personal and professional, theory and practice; making it 'real' as opposed to the sanitised 'professional' versions to be found in textbooks or practitioner research. These 'official' accounts are biased by the nature of the purpose they were commissioned for in the first place and rarely take account of the realities of practice or life itself.

Social work has, over recent years, begun to acknowledge the value of personal accounts in promoting understanding and knowledge of 'the human condition' as it relates to clients' strengths, needs, difficulties and oppression, in a number of areas, including the social work process. We rarely, if ever, hear the social worker's voice and it is time to challenge the paralysis with which we are afflicted.

Chapter 1

I was born in 1953, in Brixton, London, the second daughter of an accomplished weaver and (I was later to discover) a bent copper. Originating from the North-West of England, the family moved to London when my father transferred to the Metropolitan Police Force. I understand that my mother was madly in love, for which she paid a heavy price. My family rarely spoke of what happened in these days; however, my mother did tell me that she owned two dresses and two pairs of knickers, so one of each was permanently in the wash whilst the other was being worn. She was unable to breast-feed and couldn't afford baby milk, and so I was reared on watered-down Carnation milk, which may explain the current unhealthy state of my teeth and bones. My father, on the other hand, had to have an extensive wardrobe in order to engage in the socialising and womanising as was his wont. Later, after my mother had died, I was told by her cousin of the beatings my mother endured if there was so much as a speck of dirt on one of his crisply laundered shirts.

Much later, following the death of my grandfather, me and my sisters discovered old newspaper cuttings from the *Manchester Guardian*, documenting the trial and sentencing of my father to three years in Strangeways. I was two at the time and my mother was pregnant with my younger sister. The offence was related to importuning and had occurred in the days when homosexuality was illegal. My father had apparently hit upon a money-making scheme whereby he lured a well-to-do businessman to a hotel and, producing his warrant card, proceeded to attempt to blackmail him. He was subsequently arrested in a public phone-box when retrieving a large amount of money left there, following a tip off from the businessman and a police surveillance operation.

My mother and I returned up North, where we were reunited with my grandparents and older sister – my mother and father had agreed to her being left in the care of my gran 'until they were settled'. My mother returned to the mill following the birth of my younger sister, often working double shifts to earn enough to keep us, whilst my gran cared for us. My mum was a proud woman; she wouldn't claim benefits and never received a penny from my father. I never knew him but, around ten years after my mum died (when I was in my 30s), curiosity got the better of me and my sisters and we eventually tracked him down. He had a young partner and had allegedly made a million and blown it, was now quite affluent and didn't want to know his grandchildren, but was keen to keep in touch with us, his grown-up daughters. We didn't pursue it. We were quite sickened by him and felt nothing; also our step-dad was dying and, despite his failings, he had done more for us than our father had.

Although we felt he 'owed us' and, desperately poor as I was at the time, I couldn't compromise my principles by asking for any help from my father.

My relationship with my gran was strained; we had no contact until I was two, whereas she cared for my sisters from birth. Additionally, I was headstrong and reacted negatively to what I experienced as the preferential treatment of my sisters; hence, I was always in trouble for hitting them and/or executing various devious means of getting back at them. Being the middle child, I was often resentful because I was always told I had to make allowances for my younger sister as she was the 'baby', and similarly I had to give way to the older one because she was 'older' than me; I always thought it was an excuse and felt peeved. Generally speaking, the three of us got on well as kids; at least, as well as three sisters can when young, although we had many a set to over something and nothing as kids do. The fact that we were very close, emotionally and spatially, meant that each one of us knew what buttons to press and with whom.

I remember that we used to have small bottles of fresh orange juice delivered by the milkman on a Friday; it was a special treat. My youngest sister, Rachel, greeted me at the front door one Friday from school, when gran had nipped out to the shops, informing me that she had drunk mine (gran used to put our initials on the foil tops) and was saving hers for later. As I was about to grab hold of her, gran returned and was told by Rachel that I was taking her juice. I was stuffed. Gran wouldn't listen to any explanations and, surveying the evidence – i.e. the empty bottle and cap with my initial on it – insisted that I didn't dare drink the contents of either of the other bottles. I was furious but I didn't dare cross her, so I took Rachel's bottle upstairs, carefully prised the top off and added a generous helping of talcum powder. I knew I'd get a good hiding but it was worth it to see the look on Rachel's face when she took a swig out of it. On reflection, I might as well have just drunk it – but there you go.

At other times we could be quite co-operative, particularly if embarking on joint ventures. We used to always make a 'Guy Fawkes' for Bonfire Night and, in the days leading up, would place it over the garden wall to catch mill folks clocking on and off. We used to hide behind the wall and move one of the stones to put the collecting tin there, next to the 'penny for the Guy' sign. Unbeknown to us at the time, we were clearly visible to passers-by, as the wall was only three feet high and on a bend in the road. Afterwards, we would cart the Guy door-to-door, singing and collecting. One year we decided we needed a more lifelike Guy in order to make more money, and I think we were also on the last minute; we were aged about seven, nine and eleven at the time. As Rachel was the smallest, we dressed her up, painted her face and dragged her around in a box-cart contraption. And very well we did too until we called at a rather posh house with lots of steps up to the door and no means of getting the cart up. Not to be outdone, we left the cart and propped Rachel up against the door so the occupant could see her. We needn't have bothered as the woman came out demanding we leave her property and take that 'thing' with us. I really don't know who was more scared, us or her, when Rachel suddenly 'came to life' and lurched down the steps. Happy days, but we didn't dare tell gran because she didn't approve of 'begging'.

We were keen patrons of the local Catholic school jumble sales at the time, which were useful for dressing-up clothes and the odd handbag, etc; we were always in trouble with gran on account of the 'load of old rubbish' we'd bring back. This gave us the idea for some fund-raising of our own, on behalf of a local residential home for young people who had Down's Syndrome; me and my older sister later became volunteers at the home for a while when we were in our early teens. We held a 'table top' sale in the alley between the rows of houses where we lived, selling donated toys, books and 'good' second-hand clothes. We did extremely well, though I can't remember exactly how much money we raised, until one woman began to haggle with us over a new blouse that the woman from the wool shop had given us, still in its packaging. As I recall, it was a bargain but the woman offered us half what we asked, then stomped off shortly after we declined; within ten minutes we noticed the blouse was missing and were sure the woman had taken it. Leaving our eldest sister (Bet) in charge of the stall, me and Rachel raced around to the woman's house intending to ask her to return the blouse; she could easily have afforded to pay for it and was better off than most. To our surprise, we caught her hanging it out on the washing line. Needless to say, it was dried, back on the stall and sold for a good price within the hour. Again, we didn't tell gran for fear of being accused of stealing.

My gran, at the time, appeared quite stern and very religious, but not in a 'Bible-bashing' fashion; she was a very strong woman who attended to the family's needs meticulously, was extremely generous and remained stalwart in a crisis. Like my mum, my gran had also worked in the cotton industry, where she had met my grandfather, who was a 'knocker-upper', if you'll pardon the phrase, and whose job involved knocking on bedroom windows to waken early shift-workers with some contraption on a long pole; he also tended to oiling the factory machines and other odd jobs. Granddad was a sweetheart who would let us play and mess up as long as we were quiet. I can still remember the rows when gran came home, particularly when we had cut up her Sunday best hat to make something (I can't for the life of me think what) and sold her copy of 'The Old Rugged Cross' album to the local junk shop in return for second-hand comics.

Granddad kept hens on a plot of land owned by the people next door, who were also the landlords. Us girls used to collect the eggs and enjoyed eating them for breakfast on a daily basis. One year, whether by accident or design, some had hatched and we each adopted one of the chicks; mine was called Snowy. I loved that chick and carefully tended it as it grew, as my sisters did with theirs. We were used to eating chicken but I guess it was always prepared whilst we were otherwise engaged and it wasn't until one fateful Christmas that our chickens came home to roost, so to speak. I walked into the kitchen to find my gran plucking a chicken, having previously wrung its neck. I was horrified – it was Snowy. I cried and cried and refused to eat it or any other chicken. It got to the point where we refused to eat the eggs and eventually the hencote, hens and chicks were no more.

I went to the local primary school where I suddenly became aware that most other kids had dads and began to call granddad 'Dad', both because I wanted to be the same as my friends and because that's what my mum called him. I was bemused by my teacher's attempts to explain my family relationships, bless her; she must have thought I was confused. Money was tight and granddad had returned to work as a night watchman, aged 67, in order to boost the family income. We had decent food and handmade clothes but little in the way of life's luxuries; holidays were more or less something other people did, although I do remember a family coach trip to North Wales for the day and that granddad's one and only suit was forever christened his 'North Wales' suit; we only ever saw him in his overalls. Our sleeping arrangements were 'unusual' to say the least, though we didn't think so at the time. My mum and gran occupied a double bed in the front bedroom, with granddad in a single bed alongside. In the back bedroom, me and my sisters slept together in a double bed; in winter we had coats on the bed for extra warmth. There was a huge walk-in cupboard at one side of the bed, which was referred to by gran, and unquestionably by us, as the 'billtin'. It wasn't until we were adults we realised that the billtin was in fact built-in. Anyhow, we 'found' an old Catholic Bible in the 'billtin' and granddad told us how his family had converted to the Protestant religion out of necessity rather than choice. Apparently, the local mill owner refused to employ Catholics, as was the norm in those days, and the family were destitute.

We didn't have a bathroom; we had an outside lav, a jerry under the bed, and an old tin bath which hung on the pantry door. Friday night was bath night; a treat if ever I saw one. Gran would boil up enough hot water to fill the bath for us in turn but the only problem was that granddad was relegated to the kitchen in the evenings, so he could smoke. He never took any notice of us but, obviously, as we began to get older we were embarrassed; the crunch came one evening when granddad had a rare visitor and attempted to bring him into the back kitchen where I was ensconced in the tin bath. And so Friday night began to be known as 'slipper bath' night, when the three of us would take clean undies, towel and soap to the local slipper baths, next to the scout hut, half a mile away. Even then it didn't feel nice to be sitting in a public cubicle having a bath with God knows who in the next cubicle. Nevertheless, I suppose it was good value for a shilling and at least gave us some privacy. We were 'poor' in comparison with our friends, who tended to have bathrooms by now; most had a T.V. and many had family cars. I don't think we ever admitted to anyone about the coats on the bed though. Otherwise I had a fairly stable, idyllic childhood up to the age of ten, when my mother met and married a soldier who was AWOL at the time.

My step-dad was 23 at the time they married and my mother was 33. He originated from Middlesex, had absconded from the Parachute Regiment, and had been working laying electrical cables in the hillside, beyond the small village in which we lived. He idolised my mother and, following a year-long romance, turned himself over to the military and served a six-month sentence in jail, in order to marry her. (My mother was an extremely attractive woman and had had other offers but prospective suitors could not accept us three daughters as part of the package.) The week after they were married, my step-dad was sent to the Persian Gulf, where he was on active duty for about two years. These were harrowing times for my mother; she was in constant fear for his safety and, within six months, she had found a lump in her breast and was diagnosed with cancer. Following a mastectomy, and having been nursed back to health by my gran, my mother returned to work. We moved into a council house in a nearby village, furnished almost entirely with the second-hand contents of an old farmhouse. Even then it looked peculiar to me to see once grand, now dilapidated, pieces of furniture marooned in a council house. The previous owners even gave us candelabra!

Us children were largely protected from the significance of my mother's illness and her fears for my step-dad, but times were hard and my mum looked anxious and sickly most of the time. Nevertheless, I can remember the pleasures of having an inside loo and the luxury of not having to bathe in the old tin bath. We all had chores to complete on returning from school; mine were to clean and set the fire, peel the potatoes, make my bed and tidy the front room. Sundays were spent curled up on the settee watching black and white films; me and my mum had a penchant for 'weepies' – I have never cried watching a film since the day she died. On Fridays I went to the local youth club.

Having renewed his enthusiasm for the Army, on my step-dad's return from the Gulf he was given a compassionate posting to a nearby Territorial Army barracks as a full-time parachute instructor. As time passed, I became increasingly aware of my mother's ill health. Over the next seven years she had further surgery, chemotherapy and radiotherapy as the cancer advanced.

Life was as normal as it could be when you are a teenager, your mother is dying, your step-dad is unable to cope emotionally, and you know something's wrong but nobody says so.

When I was 14, I ventured into relationships with the opposite sex; it was fraught with dilemmas but quite innocent on reflection. I had regular lectures from my step-dad, which I recall as being of the 'never let a boy touch your breasts' variety. Pretty ironic since the thought had never crossed my mind and that, on two occasions, it was my step-dad who tried to do it. At this point in time, my mother had quite recently been rushed into hospital, packed like a fish in ice; unbeknown to me, my step-dad knew of the likely long-term prognosis for my mother, was battling with the responsibility of three teenage daughters, and had embarked on an emotional roller coaster, whilst trying to continue to work. It wasn't until much later that I understood he was engaging in a complex process of transferring his affections from my mother to me, in an effort to escape the craziness of the situation.

This was a confusing time for me; I couldn't tell my mother as she was so poorly and I became reluctant to be in the same room with my step-dad. I remember feeling slightly queasy at the thought of him sharing my mother's bed and lost respect for him for quite some time. About four weeks later, things came to a head when he asked me to bring up a cup of tea for my mother and him; I refused. After much shouting and bawling I blurted out the reason and my step-dad said he must've been drunk and mistaken my bedroom for his; I didn't believe him. After this I developed an aversion to my bedroom, couldn't sleep or feel comfortable and eventually swapped with my younger sister.

The only thing I missed was access to the airing cupboard, as I used to wash out my white school socks each evening and put them in there to dry.

I wasn't much of a scholar; in fact one of my school reports stated that 'Susan is not academic, lacks the discipline necessary for her to achieve and is unlikely to embark upon any respectable career' – quite a damning conclusion to draw regarding a young girl of 14! However, education was not high on the agenda in our house, considering the fact that my mother's ill-health caused her to give up work and we often had to hide under the kitchen table to avoid the rent man. In school I was a bit of a class clown; I suppose it provided a bit of light relief. I hated maths; it made no sense to me whatsoever and I could never grasp the significance of working out how many hours it would take for ten men to build a wall, etc. I did enjoy history lessons, chemistry and French but, because I wasn't in the top two forms, did not have the opportunity to pursue French and had to swap chemistry for general science, which I hated. I also loved to read but the 'delights' of Shakespeare and other literature such as *Three Men in a Boat* eluded me. As a working class lass they spoke to me in terms I was unfamiliar and uncomfortable with, and therefore were meaningless.

I couldn't cook, as was evidenced by the burnt offering of a Christmas cake I was made to ice and put on display with the rest of the class, to teach me a lesson. It did and I swapped domestic science for woodwork. I had no interest in staying on at school to do exams – it was never for the likes of me. It was just as well because, as with my sister who was brighter than me and wanted to stay at school, we couldn't afford it. And so I was destined, at the age of fifteen, to join my sister working as a junior wages clerk with a company in a nearby town. For my family it was a sign of upward mobility and a blissful relief that we would not be subjected to the arduous rigors of the mill.

I enjoyed the world of work and the fact that I could now go to the youth club on Fridays and afford to go dancing in a nearby town on Saturday nights. In the sixties the world was space mad; even chocolate bars were named after planets and constellations and the 'in' place to go for under-16s was the 'Moon' discotheque. I recall being home late one night after missing the bus, being asked where I'd been and receiving a well-aimed belt around the head when I innocently replied To the Moon. Despite the fact that I was useless at maths, I found no difficulty in learning to calculate wages, which was done manually at the time, including extra payments for boots and 'dirt money', but I found it less easy to cope with the two middle-aged women I shared an office with. I tried hard to get along with both; however, Jean used to make constant reference to my mother as being amongst the 'sick, lame and lazy' because she wasn't working, whilst Liz used to compare me unfavourably with her own daughter who was apparently very clever.

It upset me to think that Jean thought my mother was lazy, given all she had suffered, and I knew Liz's daughter to have had opportunities which I had not; word was that she wasn't that clever either! (I took great delight in telling Jean exactly what I thought of her during a chance encounter in the bus station at the age of 21, just after my mother died.) The crunch came the following December when I arrived two hours late for work due

28

to being snow-bound; the bus service was cancelled and I had walked the six miles from home. In the absence of the boss, Jean was 'second in command' and took no prisoners, despite the fact that my fingers and toes were blue with cold and that many employees did not turn in at all. Jean lived around the corner. I found a new job as a stock control clerk and left the following week.

I was never short of boyfriends, though at that age relationships were fairly innocent, transitory and disposable. I got on really well with Gary. We liked the same music and dancing and other girls thought he was 'cool', which made him even more of a catch. I soon chucked him back though. He bought tickets for us to see Jimmy Ruffin at The Twisted Wheel in Manchester, which was the hippest place to be at the time. Unfortunately, my parents (quite rightly) refused to let me go, despite my pleading, as it was an 'all-nighter'. Gary took someone else who was renowned for being 'easy' and I never forgave him. Having taken a full two weeks to get over Gary, I accepted an invitation to go dancing from a lad I'd met at a friend's birthday party and who lived miles away. Chris was fun to be with, good looking, and had just passed his driving test and been bought a car by his parents. I didn't tell my mum or step-dad because I knew I wouldn't be allowed to go out in a car with a boyfriend. Anyway, my step-dad had recently won some money on the horses and arranged to take my mum away for the weekend. Bet had been drafted in to keep an eye on me; she was 18 and I was 16. I think Rachel went to stay with friends, or may have gone with them, I'm not sure. At any rate, I was seeing Chris for the third time and Bet had a first date on. I had a brilliant night out, returning quite late (for me.) As we kissed goodnight in the car, Chris pressed a piece of paper into my hand; he told me it was his phone number, that I was a great girl, pretty and lots of fun, but he only gave a girl three chances to 'give'. As I stumbled out of the car in tears, he followed it up with, 'if you change your mind give me a call.'

I was devastated. I went straight upstairs to bed, as I could hear Bet downstairs with her date, and cried myself to sleep. Bet woke me up in the early hours of the morning to tell me that she was no longer a virgin. I didn't much care at the time but listened to her raving over the boyfriend anyhow. Boy, did that night come back to bite me on the arse, putting me in a Catch-22 position that I couldn't get out of. Bet was staying at gran's at the time and had only been with me for the weekend to make sure I behaved myself! On returning from their weekend break, my mum and step-dad had quite a shock when one or the other of them lit the fire. On pulling down the 'damper' (an aid to help the fire catch light, situated at the back of the fire), they were faced by the sight of a used condom stuck fast to the front of it. I received a grilling, the likes of which you've never seen, which lasted for weeks. What could I say? That it wasn't me, it was Bet? Not likely! No matter how much we squabbled, it was an unwritten rule between 'growing up' sisters that you never dropped each other in it. So I continued to deny all knowledge and was grounded for six weeks. I'm not sure if they eventually realised it was Bet because it just went away and nothing more was said; usually, if I'd done something wrong and been caught out I'd eventually own up.

Shortly afterwards, I renewed my acquaintance with an 18-year-old local boy who had enlisted in the Royal Navy two years previously; I was in love. James was tall, dark, handsome and a quiet, gentle person. I was blissfully unaware that he already had issues, which would subsequently impact upon me for the rest of my life. Needless to say, my step-dad did not approve and took to grounding me whenever James was on leave. He also hid the letters that were written to me. By this time my mother's health had deteriorated further and my step-dad had succeeded in convincing her that James was a 'bad lot' on the basis of little, if any, discernible evidence. I was miserable; I redirected my mail to a friend's house and returned from work each day to spend the evenings in my room, managing to see James once each time he came home – by escaping through the bathroom window – and paying the consequences later. In an effort to feel close to me, James sought Bet's company at weekends in the local pub but unfortunately she construed this as something more than friendship. All hell broke out when my gran and step-dad found out I was still seeing James; my gran accused me of stealing my sister's boyfriend – I never did understand why it would've been okay for her but not me. My step-dad confined me to my room; he was so angry.

Eventually my mother intervened and, at the time feeling quite well, suggested they should meet with him and judge for themselves. I recall that the four of us went to the pictures and, afterwards, my parents invited James in for a few beers. At the end of the evening, my mother having long retired to bed, I was allowed by my step-dad to say goodnight to James on the doorstep; my step-dad shook hands with him as he left. As the door closed, he hit me full in the face, knocking me to the floor. I ran upstairs into my bedroom with my step-dad hot on my heels. He asked several times whether I loved James. Each time I said yes, he hit me in the face with such force that my head bounced off the bedroom wall. If I tried to say no, he would hit me with equal force and call me a liar. The commotion woke my mother, who was horrified with the scene she witnessed; I don't know the outcome of their private discussion afterwards but I had made up my mind; I couldn't stay. I came home from work early the next day, packed my clothes, and James and I returned to Plymouth where his ship was in dock.

I wanted to get in touch with my mother but I was scared; I also missed my sisters, gran and granddad, and my friends. I found work in a local newsagent's shop and we moved into a dingy flat near the railway station, which I set about cleaning and painting within an inch of its life. About a week later, the police came to visit and subjected us to the 'contraceptive discussion'; it was academic at the time as we were both still virgins. These were bittersweet times; we had little money but were happy in a fashion. We used to buy small bags of coal from the corner shop, when we could afford it, and I was a frequent customer of local jumble sales but not for handbags and dressing-up clothes this time. I was always on the look out for other people's cast-offs and managed to turn the flat into a fairly cosy home. We didn't have a television but we used to listen to plays on the radio and joined the local library. We couldn't afford to go out anywhere but, this first Christmas, we managed to scrape up the price of half a pint of cider at the local pub, drinking it with the aid of two straws. It lasted us much of the evening and the landlord didn't seem to mind.

I was lonely when James was away. I struck up a friendship with a girl who worked alongside me in the office where I was working as a stock control clerk. Gill's fiancé was in a band and spent much of his time touring around playing gigs up and down the country. On Friday nights, Gill used to come home from work with me for tea – mostly beans on toast, if we were lucky, and we'd spend the evening together. At weekends I felt totally lost, wandering into the town and having a cup of tea in Woolworth's, before returning to the emptiness of the attic flat. I read a lot and wrote my letter to James every night, by candlelight usually as I rarely had a shilling for the meter. We decided to get married on my 18th birthday but had to delay this by two months because James was at sea. In the event, he returned home for one day, on my birthday, when the ship developed mechanical problems and was undergoing repairs in France.

I conceived my first child on this day and, having been married two months later, returned home on honeymoon to my parent's house.

Chapter 2

I was welcomed home like the prodigal daughter when I returned as a married woman, and treated very differently. My mother had taken a less strenuous job as the cook's assistant in a small factory, due to a resurgence of good health. My step-dad was working as a wagon driver, after leaving the Army, and James returned to sea when I was two months pregnant with my first child. I needed to work to save some money to furnish a home for my new family; we knew we couldn't afford to buy a house and duly applied to the local parish council to be placed on the housing list. We were in no hurry as we expected James to be given a shore base which would mean moving, possibly abroad, for two years. James had served on two aircraft carriers, each for two years and was currently touring the Far East. I was seven months pregnant the next time I saw him, which was when I travelled to Plymouth for the ship's return, amid a fanfare of pomp and ceremony. I loved him madly and was disappointed to find out that I wouldn't be able to be with him for long, as James was on duty that night and, within a week, the ship would set sail on manoeuvres, destination unknown.

I found work as a wages clerk with a local company, managing to hide my pregnancy for eight weeks. My employers were angry when they found out and I felt bad about not telling the truth, but needs must when the devil drives. I spent my evenings with my mum, step-dad and sisters and, although I continued to miss James, I was optimistic about the future and life was fairly settled. I couldn't wait for the birth of my baby and the return of my husband; in the event, James returned home three weeks before the baby was due, had minor surgery for a boil on his bum, and so was around when the baby was born. During the last few days we must've been a comical sight, as I recall being unable to stand up due to pains in my back, whilst he was unable to sit down.

I was admitted to the local nursing home early one Saturday morning; I had been in slow labour all week and so arrived just in time. At one point the ambulance stopped at the bottom of our road, as the birth was imminent, but drove off at my request because I was scared; my mother was creating a scene outside and I wanted to be in the hands of someone I saw as knowing what they were doing. There had been a fiasco at the house when I had woken up in excruciating agony, feeling the need to push urgently. My mother was reassuring James that there was no hurry as this was my first child and it could be hours of a job. James was reading aloud from a book intended to instruct fathers-to-be on how to support the mother during labour. Between the two of them, book in hand and not listening to me, they were engaged in trying to force me to sit down, have a cup of tea and relax! Never was I so glad to get out of there.

The nursing home had strict policies regarding the presence of men during labour and promptly sent James away in the ambulance in which we arrived; he had not reached home before the baby graced us with her presence. I was walking on air, as were James, my mother and other family members. This was the first baby to be born, on both sides of the family, in my generation and we adored her. It should have been a ten-day stay in the nursing home but, as James was due to fly to Malta that evening to rejoin his ship, allowances were made so that we could take baby home after four hours to be together. I was so pleased; matron would not allow me to unwrap my baby and see her fingers and toes (a pastime all but a few new mothers engage in) and it wasn't until the ninth day that you were shown how to bath your baby! My mother took a week off work to support me and to fuss like a mother hen; she was never as well as this again. Meanwhile, due to her religious beliefs, my gran would not allow baby over the threshold at her house until she was christened. Although brought up as a Christian, I had begun to be fed up with the hypocrisy of 'organised' religion and was well on my way to becoming agnostic by this time. As it turned out, given the depth of my gran's feelings, Jess was christened at the age of three months when her father returned, in order to keep the peace.

My sisters loved Jess to bits and both of them took her out, lavishing time and attention on her; Rachel took to carting her around everywhere like a handbag, much to the dismay of her friends. By then my mother's ill health had forced her to give up work and she was alternately blowing up like a balloon and losing weight at the rate of knots. I hadn't really noticed and no explanation was given, therefore I can only assume at this stage that I'd thought this was within the realms of normality, given the invasive treatments she had endured. What I didn't know was that, apart from my younger sister, I was the only member of the family not in the know.

This information came like a bolt from the blue six weeks later, as I was about to join James, who had begun a two year posting in Gibraltar and had secured a flat for rent, until married quarters became available. I already had mixed feelings about leaving my mother and the rest of the family, and had retired to bed early, as I was due to leave first thing in the morning for an RAF flight from the South of England. I was awoken at two a.m. by my step-dad and Bet, who said they had something important to tell me which could not wait. Evidently they had known for sure for a number of weeks that my mother's condition was terminal, but had resolved not to tell me. As the time of my departure grew near, my step-dad could not let me go without knowing. I was in turmoil, and we sat up for most of the night; I couldn't think straight, never mind make any decisions, and so, as if in a trance and with Jess in tow, I was shepherded onto a plane and deposited in Gibraltar with James.

In those early weeks I was distraught; as the weeks turned to months I began to settle in a fashion. We moved into married quarters and I lived for news from home. I began to 'imagine' that women I saw at a distance were my mum, that she had got better and had come to visit. When the woman would draw closer and I realised my mistake I felt miserable; my mother wasn't going to get better and how could she visit, even if well – she wouldn't have been able to afford the airfare. Life was unbearable and I turned to my James for comfort, only he wasn't there. For months now, James had been absenting himself from home, not coming home from work until late, if at all. On the occasions he did return, he was drunk; when challenged, he would become insulting and hurtful to the extent that I said I wanted to go home. I didn't understand what was happening to us and, unbeknown to me, the crutch he had been using to get him through the past two years of being apart (i.e. alcohol), had taken on a life of its own and James was firmly in its grip. It was much later that I came to fully understand; I was only 20 at the time, confused, desperately sad and lonely. After one particularly nasty encounter, I decided that I had to get away for my own sanity; James told me that I had nowhere to go, my mother was dying and serve her right, everyone knew she had been a whore. I was devastated, although James denied all knowledge of having said these things when sober. I struggled to make sense of it all and returned home with baby Jess. Although I loved James totally, I reasoned with myself that I needed to be at home to look after my mother and that the break would give James the opportunity to consider his actions and our future.

My mother was over the moon to see me, and in particular Jess. This was in early 1973 and by autumn of that year, my mum had taken to her bed never to come downstairs again until November 1974, when she was admitted into hospital for the final time. These were dark days, littered with pain and suffering, both emotional and physical. Pain relief was fairly primitive in those days and, although everyone in the family knew of the inevitability of my mother's demise, the patient was always the last to know. This was just the way it was and I hated the lies and the pretence. It could have been different but again, I was young and my trust in professionals was great. Privately, my mother knew she was dying and we all shared this unspeakable secret, aided and abetted by our family G.P. and the district nurse, both of whom in all other aspects were supportive and caring. There was no such thing as disability or caring allowances in those days, which would have made life easier for my mother, since my step-dad had taken a less well-paid job so he could be closer to home. Nor was there any such thing as the McMillan Nursing Service. Now that I was at home to look after my mum, my sisters and step-dad were more able to concentrate on work, and my gran, whose own health was not good, did not have to make the daily trip on foot with her basket of goodies to tempt her daughter to eat. She still came.

I remember having to hide the ironing in the fridge before gran arrived; my mother knew that gran would set to and iron it, so it was best she didn't know it was there.

My mother, an accomplished knitter, began to while away the long nights when she was unable to sleep by making skirt and jumper sets for Jess, which she continued to do until the month before she died, only giving up because she was practically blind and it upset her so much to feel the dropped stitches. Mum also had a two-year 'relationship' by letter, with a Manchester radio disc jockey who used to talk to her and keep her company 'on air' during the night. They would share jokes and nearly every night he would play something for his friend 'Margaret'. Me and my sisters encountered him many years later, by chance, and were delighted to hear that he remembered his friend. We were also able to tell him what a comfort he had been to her in those lonely hours.

There wasn't much to look forward to in the months to come but we made the most of what we had. Jess used to love to sit on my mother's bed, laughing, chatting and 'pretend' picking toys out of a catalogue for Christmas. During the times when mum was feeling well enough to chat, she used to tell me about her own life and times when young. She spoke of her memories during the war, although she was just 14 at the time, and of her and gran spending many nights in the local air raid shelter. Apparently, my granddad preferred to stay in his own bed on the basis of his belief that if his number was up, it would find him wherever he was. Having tried unsuccessfully to enlist in the Army in WWI at the age of 15, granddad was now peeved that he was too old to fight in WWII. His interest in battleships of the time and all things military stayed with him throughout his life.

Mum also told me about her foray into Manchester at the age of 15 with her cousin, who was 18 at the time. This was at the time that American soldiers were said to be 'overpaid, oversexed and over here'. Mum's cousin had met a black American soldier on a night out and arranged to see him again, taking my mother along as a 'blind' date for his mate. Having received the legendary chewing gum and nylon stockings, which you couldn't get hold of for love or money, it seems the soldiers were expecting a little something in return. My mother and cousin 'legged it' all the way to Piccadilly Station in order to avoid payback, though they were pleased they didn't have to continue drawing a seam down the back of their legs with an eye pencil, so it looked like they were wearing stockings.

My mum told me how naïve she was and that she really didn't know where babies came from until she had Bet; she said she was scared because she thought they came out of your belly button. Knowing gran I can fully understand this. I can also imagine that if gran had ever known of mum's escapade in Manchester she would've hit the roof. Years later, after she was divorced, Mum had met a minor celebrity at a dance. She told me that she knew who he was and that he was married, despite the fact he'd given her a load of bull. Having agreed to go out with him the following Saturday, she and my gran had sat on the window ledge in the upstairs bedroom, watching him driving up and down the road looking for a non-existent address. She thought it served him right. I still see him from time to time on the T.V; he achieved a greater degree of celebrity than in my mum's lifetime and seeing him brings back memories and makes me smile.

Mum told me about what had happened to granddad's only sister. I had seen the one and only photograph of her and could see the family resemblance to my mum. She was 35 when she died and had left three children, whom she'd never been allowed to see for a number of years. It transpired that Annie had been admitted to an infamous 'Northern' asylum following the birth of her youngest child. We now know that she would've been suffering from post-partum psychosis, but at the time she would just be considered to have 'gone mad' and incarcerated as many other women were. Annie's husband had apparently disowned her and refused granddad access to his nieces and nephews. Gran and granddad used to visit her weekly and, after the first couple of years, Annie was allowed home on weekend leave to granddad's house providing he took responsibility.

Annie 'lived' in the asylum for a number of years, even though it was felt that she was fully recovered. The problem was that, in those days, the husband needed to sign the discharge papers and this one refused, condemning his wife to a lifetime of misery. I can't imagine how she must have felt on her weekend visits, knowing her children lived just beyond the hill and yet she couldn't see them. Gran and granddad had begged and pleaded with Annie's husband to sign the papers, promising that Annie would live with them and that they would take responsibility. Gran later told me that, on Annie's last visit, she spoke of how much she loved her children and the emotional pain and suffering she experienced. Consumed with grief, Annie never returned to the asylum that day but drowned herself in the reservoir nearby. Granddad was called upon to identify his sister as they retrieved her body with grappling irons. Gran told me he was not the same person and never ever spoke of his sister again.

We had many 'hypothetical' discussions regarding life after death and the likes. My mum used these discussions to address issues we never would have talked about in 'real terms'. My family were staunch Socialists; I would have said Labour supporters, but that would be misleading as I don't see much socialism in current times. At any rate, mum said that I would always be sure it was her, should it be possible to contact anyone from beyond the grave, on account of the crude and derogatory 'password' she shared with me, regarding a prominent Conservative politician of the time. She also said, in passing, that whenever anything happened to her in the future she would leave a letter for the family.

And so daily life continued, with my mum pretending in order to avoid hurting us and us pretending for fear of hurting mum further. One of the bleakest days during this time was when I discovered my mother crying and shovelling tablets into her mouth, as she felt she could no longer go on. I had to rake the tablets from my poor mother's swollen mouth with my fingers, make tea and settle her back into bed. The cancer was ravaging every part of her body at this stage and was now invading her bones and blood. The fear of finding mum dead was never far away and, before I entered her room, I used to call out to her as I climbed the stairs; looking back I'm sure she must've known why. During all of these times James and I continued to write to each other. James was contrite and acknowledged the stress we were under. On his first night home on leave, we put our heads under the pillow to avoid hearing my mother's screams and the noise of her banging her head on the wall, as the cancer crept towards her brain stem causing excruciating headaches. Around the same time, my step-dad confessed that he had been poised with a pillow above my mother's head when she slept, on more than one occasion, but couldn't quite bring himself to do it. By this time, my proud and beautiful mother was almost unrecognisable in a physical sense, which bothered her greatly.

I could tell there was something different the day before mum died. To be honest, despite my budding agnosticism, I had prayed all along for her to get better, but had recently begun praying for an end to her pain. Me and Jess had been sitting with mum in the morning but she wasn't really responsive; mum's eyes rolled in a peculiar fashion and she seemed to be rambling and/or talking to someone I couldn't see. I asked the next-door neighbour to look after Jess in the afternoon and just sat there waiting for my sisters to return from work. I'd rung the G.P., to be told he was on holiday and spoke to the locum on call. He told me that when morning surgery was finished he would call to assess what needed to be done. He also told me not to worry. He never arrived. Much later, after I'd complained to the nurse, the doctor told her that he had never received my message!

By the time mum was admitted to the local cottage hospital late at night, there was no one on hand to administer the appropriate drugs, a situation that I had no intention of allowing to recur when my step-dad was in the same position.

Chapter 3

I'd gone with my mother and step-dad to the hospital by ambulance, when it became clear that the doctor had 'forgotten' us. It was 10p.m. when we arrived and so there was no doctor on call. The nursing staff made my mum comfortable, telling us that her lungs were filling up with fluid and that they did not expect her to last the night. My mum was completely blind at this point and unable to speak but she was conscious, able to hear, feel pain and move her fingers. I talked to my mum and told her she would be okay now that she was in hospital. Another lie, but I didn't know what else to say. I held my mum's hand and she searched for my ring finger, presumably trying to identify which of her daughters was there.

In the event, my mum died at 4p.m. the following day; her heart was strong in more ways than one. My step-dad and his sister had returned to the hospital in the morning, whilst the rest of the family waited for the inevitable news. Thankfully she had received medication by then to relieve the pain. We were at my grandparents' home when they returned. My step-dad was ashen; his sister handed me a carrier bag which I opened, unthinkingly, to reveal the clothes in which my mother had been admitted. It was like a knife piercing my heart and I began to cry and shake uncontrollably.

My gran, who had managed to stay strong for her daughter throughout all of this, took to her bed on this day and never recovered. She was too sick to attend the funeral and basically had given up; my mother had been her only child. The week in between my mother's death and the funeral passed in a fog. I don't have much recall of events that week, save the fact that none of us bathed or changed our clothes till the morning of the funeral. My mother's best friend took me to the chapel of rest to see her. She thought it would help me; she coaxed and cajoled and I would've gone along with anything at that point.

It was a big mistake, as I found the whole experience macabre and upsetting; rather than seeing my mum 'at peace', I saw a swollen, wax statue of a figure which looked nothing like her. My mum was buried with Jess's christening bracelet and other mementos from the family. James had returned on compassionate leave and, along with my step-dad, brother-in-law and my step-dad's three brothers, had carried my mother's coffin. It broke my heart.

James rejoined his ship, in Malta, two days later and I packed some belongings and moved into my grandparent's house with Jess, to care for my gran. My sisters had to work and life had to return to normal, whatever that was. My gran was extremely weak and needed to be lifted out of bed and onto the commode; she ate like a sparrow and quickly became a shadow of her former self. I followed her instructions to the letter, in making 'beef tea' to her specification; but even when I got it right she couldn't drink it. My granddad, meanwhile, could not accept that his 'Maggie' was dying and chose to believe that she had succumbed to a bad bout of 'Asian flu'! He had built his whole world, for the past fifty years, around his wife and daughter and was to lose both in the space of three months; he was a broken man.

My relationship with my gran was good at this time; in fact it had been growing strong since I had begun to care for my mother. She did once tell me that she had revised her opinion of me, when she saw how much I loved James and Jess and had looked after my mother as best as I could. Jess was nearly three now and growing fast; she was gran's constant companion along with myself. When gran was up to it, she would play 'heads, shoulders, knees and toes' with Jess, and we would sing nursery rhymes and play 'hide and seek' in gran's room. Gran told me I had enough on my plate and that, if my husband loved and respected me, he would 'leave me alone' until Jess was at least five; it tickled me that my gran had obviously not heard of contraception. I wasn't fully aware that gran's concept of sex was 'all duty and no pleasure', as with many women of her generation. Not that this was an issue anyhow; we hadn't made love in ages and James was avoiding me, but he still wrote to me with affection and had applied for early discharge from the Navy, so that we could be together as a family sometime soon.

My gran told me stories from her own childhood and about her parents and their lives. She was the second youngest child and described her father as 'a God-fearing man' and her mother as a 'saintly woman'. My maternal great-grandmother had apparently had two illegitimate children, as a result of having been 'made go with the lodger' to supplement the family income. She met my great-grandfather, a lay preacher, in the late 1870s and went on to have a further four children. Much later, obviously having been rankled by the esteem in which gran held her father, my granddad told me he was an idle bastard who did nothing but quote the Bible, whilst his wife was the breadwinner taking in washing and cleaning for folk until the day she died, aged 89.

Although I remember the emptiness I felt following the death of my mother, there was scarce little time for grieving, though I indulged in the usual feelings of anger, sadness and self-blame for some small action or inaction on my part, usually at bed-time when I found I couldn't sleep. Sometimes, if gran was settled and asleep in the afternoons, I would walk home with Jess, just for a breather. It was on these occasions that I would think about my mum, wandering into her room half expecting to see her. One of the worst things was that people would cross over the road rather than acknowledge me, on my way to and fro. People never did seem to grasp the fact that a kind word, even if it did bring the tears, was better for me than to pretend I didn't exist.

I carried on doing what had to be done and, with hindsight, was depressed for much of the time. Jess was my little ray of sunshine and, in addition to the letters I received from James, made me smile and kept me going. All the while we searched amongst my mum's few personal possessions for the letter I knew that she had left for us; we left nothing to chance, checking and re-checking pockets, handbags, etc., and eventually found it.

Remaining one of, if not the, most treasured possession I have, the content of this short but poignant letter is reproduced below:-

To Bet, Sue, Rachel, Robert, Mum and Dad.

To my three daughters who I love very much I have no money to leave, just all my love and wishes for their happiness throughout their lives because they are and have been my life for the past 23 Years. Also my husband who I love very much and who has stood by us all. And my Mother and Dad who I have always loved. No one should have any regrets when anything happens because you have all been so good to me. God bless till we meet again in a better world.

Margaret

My gran was admitted to the same cottage hospital as my mother had been, when her nursing needs and pain medication became too much for me to administer to, with the intention of transferring her to the geriatric unit. Gran was of sound mind and this was the thing she feared most; it brought back old memories of what she knew as the 'workhouse', which her own mother had worked desperately to avoid. Gran died with dignity three weeks later, the week before she was due to be transferred. I was happy for her in a sad kind of way.

I returned home to live in my mother's house and, that autumn, James was discharged. He took a job on nights at the local chemical factory, whilst awaiting the result of his application to join the Fire Service. He didn't have to wait long and was soon away again on a nine-week residential training course; I never did find out whether he stayed away at weekends by choice or design. At any rate, I know that he studied hard, passed with flying colours, and took up a position at a local fire station by Christmas. In the New Year we were offered a council house in a nearby street and I felt that I now had something positive to focus on. We had a small amount of money put by and were able to buy a carpet and other necessities, having to make do with hand-me-downs and second-hand beds. If anything could be made of nothing, I could do it; after all I'd had plenty of practice in that department. Amongst other things, I hand sewed curtains, cushions and a tablecloth from other people's cast-off material; I was in my element as I now had a home of my own. I conceived my second child soon after we moved in and was delighted to discover that my Bet was also pregnant, as she and her husband had been trying for the past couple of years; our babies were due on the same day – 4th November 1976.

Unfortunately, I did not carry the baby very well; we had a heat wave that year and I was sick all the time up to the birth. The doctor told me it was a sign of a healthy pregnancy; small compensation to me at the time. James took the opportunity to absent himself more and more, hardly ever coming home from work; having swapped one male-oriented career for another, he struggled to settle into civilian life and, unbeknown to me, had resumed drinking to some tune. I had no control over the family finances and James would never engage in discussion as to why we never had any money, his whereabouts when not at home or at work, or anything else of any significance.

By the time my second daughter was born Jess had started school. I remember that day as if it was yesterday; it was James' day off and I had awoken at 6.30a.m. and had set about cleaning the house, after taking Jess to school. I was taken to hospital via ambulance at 10p.m. that night, followed by James on his motorbike. I watched from the back of the ambulance, as we reached a fork in the road. To my dismay, as the ambulance carrying me went one way, James and his bike went the other; much later I saw the funny side of it but definitely not at the time. James eventually turned up at the hospital, and though he had evidently 'had a few' he arrived just in time to see his daughter born, on the very day she was due. I remember holding Katy up to the window the following night (5th November) to 'see' the fireworks. 'Isn't She Lovely', by Stevie Wonder, was playing on the radio; it became 'Katy's' song and even now when I hear it thirty years on, my memories of that night come flooding back.

Bet took care of Jess whilst I was in hospital and James worked. I couldn't wait to come home as I missed both of them. James came for Katy and me on the fourth day and we arrived home by taxi where my sister and step-dad were waiting. Rachel had joined the Navy herself by then and was undergoing basic training. About a week later, James announced that he had arranged to go out with the lads from the fire station to 'wet the baby's head'. I can't say I was pleased but he would have gone anyhow. He didn't return for three days; I was demented. I had a new baby, the 'baby blues', Jess needing getting to school and, to top it off, Bet had been admitted to hospital for a Caesarean section as her baby was now overdue. I couldn't face going to the hospital to see them, I was in such a state, but I knew my sister would wonder why I stayed away. I had rung the fire station, the hospital and everywhere I could think of; I had visions of James having come off his bike somewhere and lying dead in a field.

I reported him to the police as a missing person and, when he walked in as if nothing had happened, I rang the police back and went out, leaving him to make the excuses and apologies. He had apparently been on a 'bender', staying with a friend and with no thought to his family. According to James, the coppers thought it was funny! This was the beginning of the end, but it was to be a further eleven years and one more child before I had the strength, opportunity and self-confidence to extricate myself from this disastrous marriage.

I returned to work as a part-time plastic welder when Katy was six weeks old. Bet looked after Katy for me and James was supposed to take over when he wasn't working; more often than not, he would turn up at Bet's house with some excuse to leave Katy with her until I got home and he would roll in around midnight. By this time, James was an absent father and husband in every sense of the word. He took a job as a taxi driver, when not working, and I never really knew where he was. I used to tell him that no one would love him the way I did and that if I knew what was wrong we could work it out together. If I tried to touch him, he would jump away as if I'd burned him with a red-hot poker! We began to live our lives quite separately, together but alone. My return to work was a necessity in order to feed the kids and myself; at this point, James was paying the rent, utility bills and his work expenses but nothing else. Whenever I asked him for money there was none to be had. I began to feel I was a burden upon James as a result of the things he used to say to me; the once bubbly and fairly self-confident girl I used to be had begun to change, and not for the better.

My sister, Bet, has often said she could not understand how I allowed this to happen. I guess that everything I'd had to deal with up to now had left me depleted and in no position to contemplate losing any more of my loved ones. I had no money, nowhere to go, two children who were dependent on me, no one to turn to and began to feel somewhat grateful that my husband stayed with me; I was, after all, beginning to believe the things that James said to me, such as, 'Take a look in the mirror then you'll know why I don't come home from work'. He also used to comment on the cleanliness of the household, which was always good given the abject poverty we lived in. I knew nothing of alcohol abuse; few of us did in those days. James was never physically confrontational; he didn't need to be. I was kept from asking awkward questions as a result of the emotional abuse he meted out, albeit unintentionally but as a means of keeping me off his back. It worked like a charm!

It was hard work at the factory but I enjoyed the fact that I could provide for the necessities in life and have the company of other women at work. I settled to living life on a day-to-day basis, taking Jess to school, Katy to Bet's, and working mornings at the factory. I would spend the afternoons cleaning and cooking tea and the evenings with Katy and Jess. I was usually tired and, having little money for coal to keep the fire going, would be in bed for 9pm each evening. My husband became someone I used to pass on the stairs now and again. He had a responsible job which he executed admirably but outside of this he continued to act in a totally irresponsible fashion.

I remember having to hide any money I had, which was never very much, because otherwise James would take it. On one occasion I had gone outside to hang out some washing whilst keeping an eye out for the coal-man to deliver my order. James was in bed at the time as it was his day off. By the time I returned to the kitchen, James had got up and gone out – taking the coal money with him. I cried through frustration and felt sorely embarrassed turning away the coal-man, telling him I'd made a mistake and had plenty left. It snowed the following week and, when they weren't at school, I had to take the kids to Bet's until bedtime because it was freezing cold in the house.

It sounds daft now, and few people who have not been in similar circumstances would believe it, but apart from the early years before Katy was born, James and I made love only five times during the remaining eleven years of our marriage. This situation, in addition to my feelings of not being good enough for him, made me want him more; my son Adam was conceived on one of those occasions, as I was totally unprepared and had long stopped taking the pill. At the time, Bet had started to work the opposite shift to me at the factory; she had a large pram, housing her son Paul and my Katy, which she used to push the mile or so to meet me at the factory at lunchtime and I would push it home, looking after the babies in the afternoons. When I told James I was pregnant he groaned, which made me feel much better. I saw my G.P. who told me, "Let me be the first to congratulate you". It wasn't what I wanted to hear at the time.

I carried on working, wondering how we were going to survive when my baby was born. I was worried about losing my income, which barely covered our needs as it was. Katy had survived a bad winter the year before; it was freezing cold in the bedroom and, although I always wrapped her up well, her little fingers were always blue with cold. We had little in the way of luxuries, by which I mean what others would probably call basic necessities. Life was hard; I had no vacuum cleaner or washing machine at this point and washed clothes and bedding in the bath or carted it to Bet's on a Friday night. I think if I'd been given the option of an abortion at this time, I would probably have taken it. Thankfully it wasn't on offer as, by the time I was around five months pregnant, I was looking forward to the birth and had decided I would just have to work more hours somehow to make ends meet.

Adam was born in October 1978, a beautiful healthy baby and, like his sisters, was a happy and contented child. When I wasn't working, my life revolved around my three children and home. In an effort to ensure that my children had enough to eat I often skipped meals; my eating habits have remained somewhat erratic to this day, though I do try to eat healthily now. Katy can still remember the pig's liver and onion ensemble which was regularly on the menu because it was dirt cheap and made good gravy. Unfortunately, Katy hid more of it in her hand than she put in her mouth and only as an adult 'forgave' me for serving it up so often. I became a little more confident over the next two years; I had to be to hold my own at work. In those days, part-time workers didn't receive holiday pay but worked just as hard as full-time employees, so I challenged management on this issue. For my troubles, I was given the sack, or 'laid off' as the floor supervisor explained. I fought hard to retain my job on the basis of 'last in, first out' and managed to negotiate holiday pay for us 'part-timers'. Unfortunately, this meant that one of the other girls was laid off and the rest of the shift blamed me, sending me to Coventry for the next few weeks.

During this time, the company employed one or two students during the summer, one of whom, 'Susie', a sociology student, worked alongside me. I remember thinking at the time that this girl knew nothing; she used to spout sociological theories regarding 'the working class' that used to piss me off big style. On one occasion, she was going on about mothers buying too many sweets for their kids and cream cakes when they could have bought healthier foods or saved the money, paying the rent instead of being in arrears. I asked her to consider the fact that wealthier parents could take their children on holiday, buy them nice clothes, give them positive experiences and send them on school trips. In comparison, poor parents would try to 'treat' their children in less expensive ways and, in doing so, would need to 'rob Peter to pay Paul'. Despite our differences I liked Susie and, in the 12 weeks we worked together, fur flew as we debated the pros and cons of her classical education, universities being very much the domain of the middle classes at that time, as they are threatening to become so again.

One Monday in June 1980 I arrived in work as usual, only to find that management and machines were absent; the place was desolate. I later learned that the company had taken advantage of relocation grants and had packed up and gone to Wales, taking my two weeks wages and holiday pay with them! I needed to find a new job, quickly, but unfortunately none was forthcoming. Additionally, Bet's son, along with Katy, was due to start school and Bet was looking for work herself. After two weeks I found a job plastic welding just outside the city and my next-door neighbour offered to take care of Adam. I had to travel four hours a day to work for four hours but it gave me the chance to look for something else. At home, James hadn't paid the electricity bill or the rent for three months and, tired of being hounded for money that I didn't have, I put it to James that the only way out was for him to leave. He did.

We were separated for 18 months and James visited infrequently to see the children. I was kind of relieved because it meant that I could claim benefits until I found work locally, get a pre-paid electricity meter installed, and pay off the rent arrears. James moved into a dingy room near the fire station and, apart from the meagre maintenance allowance he paid, presumably continued to fund his drinking unfettered by his family. He was not a happy man and neither was his son. I claimed benefits for the next 18 months, whilst struggling with Adam's behaviours.

Little was known or acknowledged regarding ADHD in those days and I was at a loss to know what to do. Adam was, I was sure, a bright child but he was fidgety, confrontational and difficult; he would not give eye contact, refused cuddles or any attempts to pacify him, and I was at my wit's end. I enlisted the help of my health visitor in getting a nursery placement for Adam; I also accepted the offer of help, via the child and family clinic, to find out why my son was behaving in this way and what I could do about it. I thought it could be related to his father's absence, though he had never been around much, or possibly my state of mind at the time. I was worn out, desperately unhappy, depressed and extremely worried about Adam.

During the first appointment (to obtain the family history), the female child psychiatrist pulled her glasses to the end of her nose and asked, 'don't you like men?', in a haughty and sneering fashion. I couldn't believe my ears; I loved my son, as I did all my children, and I felt upset and offended by the suggestion that Adam's difficulties resulted from some form of maltreatment on my part, because I didn't like men. Now I was well aware of the impact of subconscious thoughts and feelings and how they might manifest. After all, I had the example of my step-dad to draw on. To me this was 'mother blaming' at its best and, needless to say, I didn't return.

The nursery placement enabled me to keep what was left of my sanity and gave me the energy to cope with Adam when he was at home. Whilst the girls were largely quite happy, Adam always seemed to be miserable and badly behaved. At nursery, staff told me that Adam refused to join in with activities, choosing to stand in a corner on his own. I became concerned regarding Adam's future as he was so uncooperative and I wondered if he would 'grow out of it'; by this time James had returned home and I had a part-time job nearby, running for dinners for factory workers. I also did some office cleaning for the same company in the mornings. Despite James' promises, very little had changed. We remained very poor due to James' drinking and it was only my earnings, eye for a second-hand bargain and just plain stubbornness that kept the family going. My granddad, bless him, would lend me money when we were desperate and I would have to try to borrow it from elsewhere to pay him back. It was around this time that granddad started to be a little unwell. After a visit to the local hospital for tests, granddad was proclaimed to be as fit as the doctor who saw him; he died two days later, seven years after my mum and gran.

I had never been particularly superstitious but seven-yearly intervals were to become 'the norm' in our family.

Chapter 4

My granddad had prided himself on never having had a day's illness in his life, or one that kept him from his work at any rate. After gran died, me and my sister used to walk over to the next village at least once a week to make sure he was okay and call in whenever we needed to go shopping; I can still remember the ball-ache of shopping and pushing the pram back up the hill with one child in it, one sitting on it, and one holding onto it, with the shopping loaded in a basket underneath. Granddad used to look forward to these visits, especially seeing the grandchildren, and to letters from Rachel and her visits when on leave from the Navy.

We had persuaded granddad to accept the offer of home help; bless him, he was useless around the house. 'Dad' couldn't even boil an egg when gran died and had taken to visiting the local bakery on a daily basis to buy his food and to tease the assistants. The home help was a nice enough woman, although she did take advantage of granddad's good nature. Whilst doing her chores she would 'spot' something she didn't think he was using and, granddad being granddad, he would more often than not give whatever it was to her; unbeknown to him, she was quite a wealthy woman, having been recently widowed and well provided for. Granddad used to make us laugh, as his housekeeping routine consisted of 'daubing' paint onto dirty marks on paintwork; his eyesight wasn't good by now and, to make matters worse, he used white paint when the paintwork was 'dove grey'.

Granddad also decided that it was a waste of electricity to keep his fridge plugged in, as he shopped on a daily basis, so he bought a new one and stacked tinned foods in it; he kept it unplugged, of course. He never changed the habits of a lifetime, rose at 5a.m. and retired at 6p.m.; the fact it cut down on electricity costs was a bonus. My gran had never been one for new technology; I think I inherited it from her. She used to send me to the phone box to make calls for her and refused to have a washing machine because she didn't 'trust' them. One of the first things granddad did after she died was to buy a second-hand machine that he never used, painting it navy blue so it wouldn't get dirty! Similarly, granddad wouldn't let us cook for him; he said it was a waste of gas. In some ways, after all the good meals gran cooked for him, I think he enjoyed the freedom of convenience foods and no washing up. Lord knows why he was saving his money; he had the princely sum of £600 in his Post Office account when he died. I used my share to pay off the rent arrears, as we were facing eviction by now.

On the eve of granddad's death, me and my sister had decided to take it in turns to stay with him; although not desperately poorly, or so it seemed, he suddenly seemed quite vulnerable and, when he raised no objections, we knew he really wasn't well. We brought his bed downstairs and, as James was on nights at the time, I took Jess (aged ten) with me to granddad's on the Saturday night, whilst Bet and her husband looked after Adam and Katy (aged four and six.) There was still no inside loo, so I carried the commode downstairs and put it into the pantry for privacy; there was no food in the pantry at the time as it was all in the kitchen cupboard, otherwise known as the fridge!

Granddad had been unable to eat his lunch or tea, which was unusual as he always had a good appetite and weighed in at around 17 stone. After going to the toilet and being gone some time, I tentatively called out to check he was okay. He said no, he wasn't and, after asking Jess to stay put, I went to help granddad get up from the commode. Granddad began to shake and it became clear that he couldn't see or hear me; he died then and there in my arms.

After ringing the doctor and undertaker, in a blind panic, I rang the fire station and the Station Officer reassured me he would send James home; he arrived four hours later, worse for wear and fell out with me on the way home, as I didn't agree with him that a drink would do me good. So James went off to the pub whilst I returned home alone and in tears; the younger kids were asleep at Bet's by then and Jess stayed with a neighbour. I had no idea that James could hardly deal with what went on inside his own head, never mind be there for me. I wasn't so sad when granddad died; he was nearly eighty and he missed gran and my mother terribly. He used to tell us that he could 'see' her sitting in her rocking chair, though went to great pains to say that he knew she wasn't really there. I often pass the house of my childhood, trying to pluck up the courage to ask the owners if, one last time, I could stand in my 'bedroom' looking out onto the allotments and just soak up the feelings and memories located there; perhaps tomorrow I will.

Following the funeral, there were the usual tasks to complete, such as emptying the house. There was nothing of much material value; after all, who wants a navy blue washing machine? At this point I'd managed to acquire a second-hand 'twin-tub'. It wasn't much to look at, I'll grant you, but it functioned and I was grateful for small mercies. Granddad used to say there's nowt so funny as folk and, as we were disposing of his worldly possessions one day, this phrase came to mind. Answering to a knock on the door, me and my sisters were surprised to see a stranger, who offered her condolences. She said that she didn't know granddad but had often passed by during the summer and 'let on' to him as he sat in the doorway, with his radio on the 'card table' in front of him. We were touched by what she had said, until she followed it up with, 'I always liked that card table and I wondered if you wanted to get rid of it'. I don't know if we wanted to laugh or cry; I think we did both. What with that, and the fact that granddad's wallet was empty when it was returned from the undertaker, even though he had drawn two weeks pension two days previously; we agreed it probably wouldn't do 'em much good.

Over the next few years, I concentrated on work and the kids; I did move back into my step-dad's house after another hurtful episode with James. There were so many that it's hard to remember them all but by then he was almost a lodger. I didn't stay long at my step-dad's; he was long-distance wagon driving at that time. I remember that it just didn't feel comfortable and I had concerns about the girls, which I hardly dared verbalise. Jess was 13 at the time, and so I returned home. I continued to work at the factory, cleaning the offices and doing the dinner run. I had learned to manage the all-male workforce who, believe me, gave me a run for my money, but by now I could give as good as I got. I also took a part-time job, three afternoons a week, doing some cleaning for a woman in the village; over the years the job became less and less cleaning and more acting as companion/carer to her mother who lived in a 'granny annexe'.

Sophie had suffered a series of strokes and I used to play word games with her to try to encourage her speech. She always wanted to give me a hug, which was funny, since according to her daughter, she was a titled 'Lady', had always been a snob and, if well, probably wouldn't pass the time of day with me. I remember thinking 'how the mighty have fallen' but, over the years, I became very fond of her and my relationship with her daughter, my employer, continues to this day.

Things became easier at home since I was now earning enough to keep us, the kids were now all in school, and even Adam's behaviours became more manageable. Of course, James continued to live as he had and I became accustomed to the fact that he was an 'outsider' in his own home. The kids never really questioned where their dad was; they were used to him not being there. Family activities, such as picnics or other 'cheap' treats, were always undertaken with my sisters, brother-in-law and nephew. Bet took the kids away on holiday with her and little by little my confidence improved. I decided I would get myself an education and enrolled at the local adult education centre for 'O' level English language and English law. I knew I didn't want to carry on doing the work I had been doing and, besides, I began to suffer from arthritis in my spine, as a result of a sledging accident with one of the kids.

I had consistently requested to see the headmaster at Adam's primary school and just as consistently been told by him that my worries about him were unfounded. The head told me there were no difficulties in managing Adam's behaviours and that, whilst not very bright, he could read, write and spell very well; I thought it must be me. Whilst Adam was not a 'naughty' child in the conventional sense, nothing ever seemed to please him. He had a very short attention span, rushing dizzyingly from one activity to another. I spent all afternoon one Saturday, for example, making him a 'Superman' dressing-up costume, whilst he whinged and whined over the time it took, only to find he didn't want it now, he wanted a 'Batman' outfit instead, and the whinging and whining started over.

Outside, Adam became the 'fall guy' for his friends' wrongdoing, as a result of his apparent 'inability' to think for himself. He seemed unable to work out other people's motives, something he has only just begun to get to grips with at the age of 28. Over the years we have spent many hours discussing the distinction between the word 'friend' and what it actually means.

Adam also developed very rigid ways of interacting with his environment; things had to be routinely ordered and predictable. He seemed unable to consider anything from anyone else's point of view, which continued until Adam was well into his late teens. It was many years before I discovered that Adam spent much of his time at school consigned to the playground wall by his teacher, preferring to be considered naughty rather than thick. It was discovered at secondary school that, although he read and wrote well, almost all of the time he had no comprehension whatsoever. Adam was bright and had developed some very sophisticated strategies to mask his difficulties; unfortunately, in other areas, these strategies were extremely dysfunctional and Adam refused help. I took some advice and decided to work on Adam's strengths to try to improve his self-confidence and break down his defensiveness. Adam took some guitar lessons from a friend of the family and continued to play snooker, for which he had a tremendous gift; whilst maths was a complete mystery to him, he could work out trajectories almost 'by instinct'.

Flushed with success at having got grade A's in my exams, I continued to study further; at the age of 32, I joined the sixth form at my old school for two afternoons a week to study sociology and psychology, mainly because it was free. I remember the feeling on encountering my 'old' science teacher on the stairs. Thankfully, I don't think he recognised me and, secretly, I thought to myself that, 'being all grown up now', why should I need to fear him? Following this, I went to various centres, gaining a total of seven 'O' levels and two 'A' levels, seven of which were grade A. At the same time as I was gaining confidence in my intellectual ability, I had a growing feeling that I needed to move on emotionally from James and I needed a decent job in order to provide for the children; I wanted to go to university. Now this may seem strange but, in my family, anyone who had a cap and gown was highly revered, whether they deserved it or not, and considered the next best thing to

God. I still wasn't sure I was 'worthy' but I knew I'd give it my best shot.

During the summer holidays I had an affair with someone I had met after night school one evening; it didn't last long. I thought I was 'in love' again, but really I think I'd been in an 'emotional coma' for so long that I was ripe for the picking, so to speak. I don't regret the affair; he was much younger than me but he taught me how to love again. Daniel was kind and caring, and insisted that he would be around forever. Of course, James heard the rumours and the guy backed off due to pressure from his parents; it gave me the kick-start I needed to file for divorce. I still see Daniel from time to time. He went on to make a bad marriage himself; he has since confided that he should have taken a stand with his parents and not passed up the chance he had been given. It was obviously not to be. This was the first and only time that James had attempted to hit me. He grabbed me by the hair and tried to 'frogmarch' me to Daniel's house. Of course, it was all over by then; I had made my mind up that I wanted out and now had the confidence to go through with it.

I visited the local DSS office to appeal for help; since I'd told James of my intentions he had stopped paying the rent and 'feeding' the electricity meter. It was Christmas Eve and we had little food or money and no presents for the kids. I was dispatched from the office with a form for James to sign to confirm that he was no longer providing for his family. I was told that an emergency payment might be made if I could return before 4p.m. The clause at the bottom of the form 'writ large' stated that failure to support the family may result in prosecution. Needless to say the form remained unsigned. In the event, I took the kids and we slept on the floor at a friend's house for six weeks until the court ordered that James should leave the family home.

James had left me a letter, which was half apologetic and half angry. In it he stated that he had always loved me and the children, and that he thought things had been getting better. He was probably referring to the fact that I no longer nagged or chased around after him and was leaving him to his own devices. He also said that he blamed himself for the way that he had treated me, that he had loved me for 'my innocence' and hated himself for taking it away. It explained the physical difficulties in our relationship but gave no indication of the complex psychological reasons which I knew must underlie his thinking; although I was aware that, when he was quite young, when going ashore the sailors were shown detailed photographs of rotting penises and issued with condoms. I can only assume that this had a devastating effect on his psyche.

It was at this point that my step-dad renewed his interest in me and began to monitor where I was going and with whom.

Chapter 5

My step-dad was somewhat bemused and amused at my desire to go to university, reinforcing the view that academia wasn't for 'the likes of me'. This view was also prevalent amongst my immediate community on the estate where I lived. Although no one said as much to my face, I knew that I was the focus of local gossip. On the one hand, it was said that I should be concentrating on Adam, since he obviously had problems, and on the other hand rumour had it that I was having an affair with my step-dad and had been seen kissing him by my front window. I had a visit from the local duty social worker, following malicious reports that Katy had been beaten. I can still remember the humiliation of that evening, as I insisted he look at each of my children, even getting Adam out of bed. In doing so, I took the social worker through the house, cringing at the sight of the boarded-up window at the back, lack of carpets, bed linen and the general poverty of the household. I felt ashamed at being so poor.

It's a funny thing but people don't always react favourably to others who, according to their perceptions, have 'ideas above their station'. I lost a number of friends at this time and left a few behind voluntarily. People who have nothing feel threatened by someone who wants to try to better herself; on reflection, I was probably the poorest amongst us and, as such, the easiest target. Later, whilst at university, I was to have visits from the DSS in response to reports that I had a new partner living with me. Ironically, I was not claiming benefits as I had a grant, but the fraud investigation team had not bothered to check before visiting. It was a while before I cottoned onto the fact that my alleged 'cohabitee' was in fact a short-haired female friend who used to visit on a regular basis.

Throughout this period, I struggled to support the children through the minefield of their own emotions regarding the 'loss' of their dad and the impact of James' inability to contain his own emotions, which he allowed to contaminate his relationship with the children. James continued to drink to excess and to avoid contact with the kids; to James, as with many absent fathers, we were a package and he could not face seeing them because of the association with me. Adam would see his dad locally, either on his way to or from the pub, and James would arrange to see him on Saturday mornings. I can see Adam now, armed with his snooker cue, going off to see his dad, only to return ten minutes later full of anger and distress as his dad had already left for the pub. Of course, I was left to deal with the fall-out, which was long and protracted. It was to be a long time before Adam gave up on chasing his dad, substituting his 'hero worship' for a more realistic view. It was agony to watch him and to be able to do very little, especially since, on the odd occasion he managed to catch up with his dad, James would fill his head with suggestions that his mother was a 'slag'. As a result, Adam would monitor my comings and goings as much as his father and my step-dad, fuelled by the rumours circulated by people who had nothing better to do.

At a time when I had been developing some measure of self-confidence, what with everything else I had to deal with, I felt depleted. My 'nerves' were beginning to suffer again. Of course, I was able to rationalise; I knew 'myself' and that what people said about me was untrue, but was unable to explain much of this to the kids, especially Adam, in a way that they fully understood at the time. In receipt of so much negativity I had a hard job to focus on the positives. Nevertheless, I enrolled on an 'A' level Psychology course, which was over two years, one night a week, at a local college; at the same time I studied for 'A' level Sociology one afternoon a week at my old school. I continued to work at the factory every morning and in a 'caring' capacity three afternoons a week. Although we had enough money for essentials, I often had to walk the four miles back from night classes, as I only had bus fares for one way. Around the house, I continued to make do and mend and it still upset me having to glue the soles of Adam's school shoes to stop them from flapping as he walked up the street. It came to the point where all three needed shoes which I was unable to buy; I was also behind with the rent and catalogue payments. That week I bought three pairs of shoes, left the rent, accruing further arrears, and left myself open to the unwelcome attention of the council rent man.

I knew for a fact that my neighbour had come to an 'arrangement' with the rent man; in return for certain 'favours' he would give her extra time to pay. I hated the sight of him, preying on vulnerable people and, let's face it, not even paying for the privilege! When he did call to give me the 'buying Johnny a new pair of shoes and not paying the rent isn't a good idea' routine, I was ready for him. It must've been obvious from my demeanour that I wasn't about to enter into any arrangements with him, or maybe he had enough willing females on his rounds – who knows! At any rate, I promised to catch up over the next 12 months and he departed quite quickly. His parting shot was to comment on how pleasantly surprised he was that the house was nice and clean!

My step-dad would conspire to visit, on the evenings I was at night school, on his way to the pub. He would also wander down the street on his way home and, if the light were on, would knock on and come in for a brew. It would never be made obvious that he was checking up on me; it didn't need to be, as it was the only time that I wasn't at home with the kids. I always felt quite nervous around him, due to the historical issues and the rumours, but he was also very good with the kids and had bailed me out financially on many occasions. All in all my step-dad's bad qualities were more than outweighed by the good, but he still made me feel uneasy. The dynamics of the relationship had changed since James was no longer around.

I had also become a volunteer at the local youth club which the children attended on Friday nights; they didn't seem to mind me being there and we had some great times. We entered a float in the local carnival – Michael Jackson's 'Thriller' – and spent hours making costumes and scenery out of something and nothing. The kids loved it. As time passed, I gradually caught up

72

with the rent and other payments and became debt-free, although we were still living hand-to-mouth in many ways. Every now and again I was able to go out with friends from night school or with my sister Bet, subject to the scrutiny of my step-dad regarding where I was going and who with. My step-dad began to have health problems and had recently had an X-ray, which revealed a shadow on his lung; at this point we had all believed it to be associated with the fact that he had contracted TB as a child.

Following extremely favourable exam results, I decided to defer application for university until the following year. I wanted to wait until Adam went to secondary school and the girls were 13 and 17 respectively, as I knew that I would have to leave the house before them and would not be home when they returned. If I was to commit to a three year course, there was much planning and organisation to be done. In the intervening period I set about preparing the kids for what was to come, took a Saturday morning job in a local shop, and began scrimping and saving for driving lessons, which I knew I would need in order to get a decent job. In the autumn of that year I received a phone call at work, which again turned my life upside down.

My step-dad had told us that he was going into hospital for an 'exploratory' examination, since his condition had not been relieved by antibiotics. Unbeknown to us, he had actually been admitted for surgery to remove part of his lung, due to cancer, and had been carrying his burden alone for some time. Due to post-surgical complications, he had an emergency tracheotomy and was currently in intensive care; the hospital was miles away, the kids were due home from school, we had no transport and the bus routes were impossible. Having negotiated these difficulties, me and Bet arrived at the hospital to be told there were no guarantees. The next 48 hours were purgatory, but my step-dad eventually recovered sufficiently to move to the surgical ward and to receive visitors.

Rachel managed to get some compassionate leave from the Navy and we set about devising visiting, childminding and other rotas. Initially, this meant taking unpaid leave from work, which obviously caused added financial difficulties; later, we managed to get a transport rota off the ground, involving everybody and anybody who could help, so that I could return to work and visit in the evenings. Most of all, I think we suffered from the shock of it and many of the familiar feelings of dread resurfaced. Aware of the ongoing effect of their father's absence, I was concerned about the impact on the kids that news of their granddad's illness would have.

My step-dad, Robert, was discharged from hospital to live with Bet and her husband, since she had a spare bedroom and was working part-time. It was not easy for Bet as Robert could be hard work at times; he could be extremely opinionated, had a 'live by the sword, die by the sword' approach to life, and felt it his place to 'toughen Bet up', otherwise he feared for her future. He might well have, though we didn't realise it at the time! Again, with the passage of time, life resumed some sense of normality. Robert had to undergo a two-week period of chemotherapy in hospital and, after the first visit, gave strict instructions not to visit again as the chemo made him sick and he wasn't up to it. Secretly we knew that he was trying to protect us from the pain of seeing him like that. It didn't work. Following this, Robert seemed to recover slowly. Together, we all set little tasks for him to complete in order for him to remain positive and to give him something to do. One of these was to meet me halfway from work at lunchtime, on the bridge over a stream; his progress was slow and painful. I used to sit by the bridge until he got there, watching out for him, feeling anxious and agitated. I think I knew what the outcome would be, but told myself not to be negative and that I could be wrong.

Gradually, Robert's condition seemed to deteriorate and, although follow-up scans showed the lung surgery to have been successful, he lost weight, became lethargic and complained of a 'frozen shoulder', for which he was treated by his G.P. Bet tried to encourage him to eat, but Robert remained highly critical of her cooking; he spent much of the day lying on the sofa, only getting up when I called at lunchtime with a salad sandwich I'd bought from the local shop on my way home. I would spend a half-hour with him before going to my second job, returning after tea with one or other of the children. I had started driving lessons by then, but had given up when the instructor told me I was getting worse instead of better. I had tried to persevere to take my mind off things but knew I was unable to concentrate. Instead, I attended a night class to learn self-hypnosis techniques for relaxation; although unable to relax due to the circumstances, looking back, these classes helped me achieve some degree of respite from the situation and to save my sanity.

By the time Robert was recalled to the hospital for the results of his brain scan, the writing was already on the wall. For weeks there had been signs of both physical and mental deterioration. Robert had been prescribed liquid morphine, which made him unwell, and he refused to take it. He continued to walk up to the pub in the evenings, dragging one leg and an arm along with him. One of us would usually make an excuse to walk up with him; it was pitiful to watch him attempt to cross the main road but he was determined. He used to make jokes about joining the 'ministry for silly walks'. Having helped Robert to make a claim for mobility allowance, it was around this time that a doctor arrived to make his assessment. I think he was in the house for all of about ten minutes and the assessment consisted of asking Robert if he could walk from one end of the room to another. Robert really didn't understand the purpose of the visit and, being a proud man, put on his best performance, walking and talking himself out of eligibility. Sadly, within two weeks he had all but lost co-ordination of all of his limbs.

In the pub, Robert caused havoc. Unfettered by the usual norms of behaviour which a healthy brain dictates, Robert could hardly stand when sober, never mind when under the influence. He often became argumentative but, thankfully, most of the clientele were aware of the circumstances and would often appease him, buying him a whisky to anaesthetise him. And themselves! For our part, me and Bet spoke to the landlord, telling him that we would pay anything that was owed. We later discovered that Robert had left a small amount of money behind the bar, weeks beforehand, in order to pay towards his wake – Robert was born in a small village in Southern Ireland and had come to England at the age of 14. He had never forgotten his roots and, thanks to Robert, we had learned of the devastation of the potato famine and the oppression of the Irish people (largely at the hands of their fellow countrymen), through personal accounts of historical events and circumstances which had been passed from generation to generation.

I had a phone installed so the landlord could let me know when Robert was leaving the pub. The traffic on the main road was horrendous and, coupled with his crippled, awkward gait and increasing lack of awareness, meant that Robert was an accident waiting to happen; we also knew that, if he fell, he was unlikely to be able to get up again. At the same time, Robert was a very proud man and we knew that it would upset him greatly if he knew he was being 'supervised'. Consequently, I would watch him coming home, hiding behind parked cars along the way, then do a short-cut over the field back to my house in case he should call, which he did often. On these occasions his mood could be quite dark and I would devise strategies to prevent him from talking about how he and I could get married, as we were not blood related.

At other times Robert could be aggressive about what he thought I might be 'up to', or be laughing and upbeat regarding something either totally incomprehensible or unfunny. My son has vivid memories of watching *The Man With Two Brains* together with his granddad, who confused him by his manic laughter during the 'serious' bits of the film. At the same time, my ex-mother-in-law had been diagnosed with some form of dementia; I can recall in detail one wonderfully nonsensical afternoon spent with the two of them in Bet's front room. Dolly and Robert whiled away the time talking to one another and laughing, totally oblivious to the fact that neither of them was making any sense whatsoever, either to us or to each other. The desire to be sociable and to interact remained strong, even whilst speaking gobbledegook.

I went to see the consultant with Robert, when he was told that he had multiple, inoperable brain tumours. Robert responded by asking whether physiotherapy would help for the 'frozen shoulder'. My head was spinning as we returned to his sister's place; she ran a pub quite close to the hospital, where Robert stayed for the weekend. Whilst the rest of us tried to come to terms with the finality of the situation, we wondered how much of it Robert understood. Given the nature of his illness, there was no point in discussing it with him and we resolved that he should live as he wished for the few weeks he had left. This meant telling his sister to 'butt out' when she, albeit well-meaning, expressed concern regarding the amount Robert was drinking, causing him to become distressed and unhappy.

Robert agreed to take morphine in tablet form, as they didn't make him sick, and, to some extent, we entered Robert's disjointed nonsensical world whenever we were with him, in an effort to make the next few weeks as palatable and stress-free as possible for him. The pressure on Bet and me obviously increased as a result; Bet's husband was a treasure and supported us fully as we took turns to go to the pub with Robert each evening whilst the other two looked after the kids. A couple of Robert's friends joined the 'rota', thank God, as neither of us really wanted to be in the pub and both of us had to go to work. Thankfully, Robert had taken to sleeping during the day. His expressed thoughts, feelings and behaviours became more bizarre over the next two weeks, necessitating closer supervision of him. He did, however, have periods of amazing lucidity and clarity in which his sense of humour shone; during one such episode, he wryly requested that we make a list of things we wanted and he would order them 'on tick'.

I had joined a local single women's group by this time and been given information about a 'singles night' at a rugby club some distance away. I desperately needed to get one night's respite from all of this and Bet encouraged me to go, along with the rest of the women. Robert was furious, calling me a slut and treating me to a tirade of insults and false allegations, including stating that I was responsible for my mother's death, as I had broken her heart when I ran away with James. My younger sister Rachel helped me to see sense at this point, as I could feel my pent up emotions about to let rip. She took me to one side, encouraging me to see that this was neither the time nor place and that if I did not regain control I was likely to regret it. She was right and I am eternally grateful to her for her observations. I did go to the 'singles night' and I suppose I enjoyed it, in terms of the company and the opportunity it afforded to escape reality, albeit temporarily. I won a huge teddy bear in the raffle to raise funds for a machine used to deliver pain relief to terminally ill patients; this machine would have special significance to me in the not too distant future.

Cheryl, an old female friend of Robert's, had helped us tremendously in keeping his spirits up no matter what; for there were many people who avoided him and us out of fear of the unknown. On one particular night, Robert had taken a taxi to his local pub to meet up with friends who had said they'd be there but weren't. The landlord rang to tell us he was sending him home in a taxi as he was complaining of excruciating pains in his head. We had to send for the doctor on call as Robert was writhing in agony when he arrived and, although he received a morphine injection, he continued to moan in pain whilst cradling his head. Cheryl came around with a bottle of brandy and her own special brand of merriment, which involved flashing her suspenders and doing the cancan, both of which Robert lapped up until the mixture of the brandy and morphine allowed him to sleep. We were all totally exhausted by then and fell asleep for a few hours on the floor where we lay.

Robert took to his bed at Bet's quite quickly after this night, experiencing a variety of delusions and hallucinations. We called his G.P. out on the second day, as he seemed to be experiencing difficulty in breathing. The doctor confirmed that Robert's lungs were filling up with fluid, as my mother's had, and that this was the beginning of the end. In consultation, we decided that it would be best for Robert to be admitted to hospital for the final few hours; the reasons were twofold, in that we wanted him to be pain-free and also did not want Bet to become any more agitated than she already was. She started to clean the house obsessively at this point and was distracted and totally immersed in her chores. Bet later told me that she had never believed that what was happening was real at any point, and had not recognised the deterioration in Robert; I was shocked on realising that Bet had subconsciously disassociated from this particular bit of reality in order to protect herself.

Whilst arrangements were made to admit Robert to hospital, the family sat talking to him and holding his hand; I noticed that this once strong, proud man had soiled himself and, although ill and in pain, was aware of it. I gave Robert some more of his morphine tablets, at intervals, and when the ambulance eventually arrived, Robert was pain-free and falling asleep. I was a bit sharp with one of the medics, for which I was sorry later, as they kindly referred to him as 'old-timer' when putting the stretcher onboard. 'He's 47', I said, gruffly, following it up with a request not to resuscitate. I couldn't bear the possibility that attempts might be made to prolong the agony further for him. I looked at Robert's emaciated body as the ambulance crew moved him,; he was around four-and-a-half stone, and I wept inside. At the hospital, I lied to the doctor who asked had Robert had any morphine today and watched as she set up the machine which would deliver timed, measured doses into his poor tortured body.

Robert died peacefully later that day, seven years after granddad died, surrounded by his family and friends; he never regained consciousness.

Chapter 6

Robert's death was a particularly sad and moving affair. In one way it was a blessed relief and brought with it some degree of closure. When he had married my mother, a divorcee, he had been excommunicated from the Catholic Church and had remained so up until my mother's death. At the same time, when my mother became ill she had converted to Catholicism, been received with open arms and been comforted by the regular visits from the priest and nuns; a situation which, to me, beggared belief. Following my mum's funeral, Robert was contacted by the priest in order to welcome him back to the fold; to my knowledge he did not return to the church in body, though what his private relationship with his God consisted of, I will never know. My step-dad received the Last Rites at the hospital and was buried alongside my mother. Thankfully, his sister paid for the funeral as we had no money and Robert had no insurance.

When we had finished sorting through Robert's belongings, we cried at the sight of such a young man's worldly possessions, which fitted into a small suitcase. Some of these things we hadn't set eyes on since my mother's death 14 years previously.

I took charge of my mother's wedding ring and a cheap plastic St. Christopher of Robert's, which he used to have in whatever vehicle he drove. I had to have the ring cut off my finger a few years later and, regretfully, I lost it. The St. Christopher has remained with me over the past twenty years, stuck to the dashboard of whatever vehicle I have driven. Other items of sentimental value were shared between my two sisters. Bet's son Paul, aged 11, wanted to keep his granddad's 'Red Beret', which was buried with Paul some seven years later.

The children took their granddad's death quite badly, Adam in particular, who was nine at the time; he went missing for two hours and was found hidden in a neighbour's hedge, heartbroken. Adam had had a particularly close relationship with Robert who, after all, could be relied on to be there for him when his father was not. In fact, we were all devastated as our family, already much diminished, now consisted of us three sisters and our children; we were 37, 35 and 33 respectively. In terms of blood relatives, following my granddad's death when I was 28, my oldest living relative was my sister, aged 30, apart from some distant cousins much removed. As a result, we were extremely close, my elder sister being 'second mum' to my children and me 'second mum' to Paul.

By the time I applied to go to university, Bet and her husband had agreed upon an amicable separation and had shared care of Paul; Robert's illness had placed a great deal of stress upon both of them. I remember the university interview as, initially, quite uncomfortable. I arrived looking smart but, on reflection, overdressed, and was greeted by the admissions tutor, who was much younger than me and looking very relaxed in his jumper and jeans. According to the tutor, I had the qualifications deemed necessary but the proverbial fly in the ointment was the fact that maths was not one of them. I knew fair well that, in such circumstances, it was likely that I would have to take a maths test; me being me, I blurted out that I would have no chance and, producing the statistics coursework from the 'A' Level Psychology course, tried to convince him that I would be able to complete the course. It worked and I was offered a place for the following September.

I had mixed feelings; I was thrilled but also knew it would be hard work whilst caring for the kids and secretly wondered whether I would be up to it. Some of my old feelings of self-doubt crept back, even down to the fact that I had rarely been as far as the city throughout my life, never mind commuting on a daily basis. I also worried about whether I could balance studying with my children's needs, reinforced by the eagerly reported comments of others, such as 'who does she think she is?' and 'she should be concentrating on her kids' education'.

Nevertheless, in September 1989, and with much trepidation, I arrived to take up my place on the BSc (Hons) Psychology course, having negotiated the many and varied pitfalls of the benefits and grants system. There were a handful of other 'mature students' on the course, which helped me to feel a little better; the majority of students were 19-year-old sons and daughters of doctors, lawyers and other professionals. It didn't take long for me to begin to feel 'at home' due to the common interest and the fact that they had little money either. I studied hard, considering it to be work for which I was paid. During term-time, I was out of the house from 7am until around 6pm due to the punishing public transport timetables, but I never wasted a minute. I spent lunchtimes in the library with colleagues and used travelling time to study, make notes and plan written assignments.

I was driven by my enthusiasm not just to pass exams but also to learn and to understand, completing coursework during term-time so I could spend much of the holidays at home with the kids. On Wednesdays I had two cleaning jobs to supplement the family income, as classes finished at lunchtime for private study. I often took Wednesday mornings off, copying the notes of a girl who took Friday afternoon off for the same reasons, when I returned the favour. I also took up the offer from a young male student of tuition on the statistical component of the course, in return for my assistance on other elements that he had difficulty in getting his head round.

During the time I attended university, both on this occasion and later when studying for a social work qualification, my sister and children used to make fun of my housekeeping routine, which was fairly non-existent. During the holidays I worked part-time in a local residential home for older people, as I was ineligible for benefits, and would 'blitz' the house; the state of the house sometimes got me down, especially since I was cleaning for other people whose houses were cleaner before I started than mine was when I finished! On Fridays I got off the train one stop before mine in order to do the shopping, lugging it home on the bus later.

In the first year, I met Martin, whom I married much later. I had known Martin for many years, since he lived in the same village. I had gone for a drink in the local pub with Bet and he invited me to his work's Christmas 'do'. It put me in a blind panic. I remember my sister telling me that he wasn't asking me to sleep with him 'for Christ's sake' and that I should go. I had a really good time and began to see him on a regular basis after this, but remained very wary, given past experience, and introduced him slowly and carefully to the kids. Martin was extremely supportive, even doing the ironing for me so I could study; rightly or wrongly, I made it clear that for the relationship to survive he would have to accept that my children and studies would have to come first. I didn't mean to make him feel second-best, but that was just the way things were. Martin accepted this and, despite the many ups and downs that were to come, we survived as a couple.

It wasn't easy from the off. Martin had been married previously, was six years younger than me, he had no children of his own, and no brothers and sisters. At the time, Jess was 17 and Katie and Adam were 15 and 12 respectively. I was determined that this was to be a positive relationship with my children or it would have to go. Martin tried hard within the realms of his own experience, although there were many heated interchanges along the way. Martin had to deal with the fact that he would never have children of his own and, with my support, learned that the relationships he made with the kids was more important than the biology. This brought a tear to his eye quite recently when on Father's Day, he received a card from my now 'grown-up' children to 'someone who is like a father to us'.

During the second year, Bet had married an Army paramedic who had promptly been posted to the Gulf. I had been concerned about her for some time, as she was getting more and more anxious and withdrawn, and had taken to being obsessively glued to the half-hourly news bulletins both at home and at work. By the time she agreed to see her G.P. she was displaying some fairly disturbing symptoms and I felt out of my depth. Bet would call at my house before going to work, talking of bizarre thoughts and feelings, and seemed unaware of anything save her own 'internal' world. Bet began to systematically cut herself off from her loved ones, especially her son Paul; unresolved feelings of loss surfaced and, whilst it seemed clear to me that she was afraid of losing her husband and son, Bet was resistant to acknowledging the cause of her distress.

Bet became deeply depressed, began to experience burning sensations throughout her body and physical sickness, and had to give up work due to her inability to concentrate; the GP's response was less than helpful and Bet left the surgery with a prescription for anti-depressants and the suggestion she 'get herself a teddy bear' whilst her husband was away! The next few weeks were hell. Bet's condition continued to deteriorate and she expressed suicidal thoughts; I felt unable to cope. I took Bet to the hospital one evening, saying anything and everything to get her there. I was afraid that she would refuse to stay and knew that she needed to. During the assessment with the on-call psychiatrist, I gave it my best shot and Bet was duly admitted, though I had to use all my powers of persuasion to keep her from walking away.

Bet remained in the psychiatric unit for a period of three months, during which time I was extremely worried about her as her condition deteriorated. I visited her each evening en route from university, taking taxis and lifts when I could get them or finishing earlier in order to get home at the usual time for the sake of the kids. I also had to explain to Paul the nature of his mum's illness and ensured that he continued to be a part of our household whilst his mother was in hospital. This also placed strain on the family finances and I was unable to study, as I would have liked to. I resolved that, in the short term, I could catch up with both.

At the same time, my eldest daughter became pregnant and she and her fiancé decided to get married sooner rather than later and moved into her in-laws house whilst they saved for a mortgage deposit. They got married 'on a shoestring' in December that year with me doing the catering; Bet's husband came home in time for the wedding and Bet was allowed home for the weekend. Much discussion took place, as Martin wanted to attend. In the event I decided it was more trouble than it was worth as, obviously, James would be there and this was Jess's day. It was funny at the rehearsal, I later heard from Jess, as I wasn't required to be there. The vicar, being friendly and not knowing the family circumstances, asked James whether his wife was well. James apparently told him, frostily, that he didn't know – he hadn't seen her for some time. Somewhat more amusing, though I didn't think it at the time, was the fact that James invited the customers in the pub downstairs at the reception to help themselves to the buffet; I was totally skint at the time and was relying on the leftover food to feed us for the following week, until the next instalment of my grant came through.

When Bet was discharged from hospital, her husband was posted to Catterick. It was to be a further two years before she fully recovered and I remained worried about her throughout. Her husband was extremely patient and had to cajole, encourage and generally do whatever he could to get her to go out and to resume normal day-to-day activities. Bet used to ring me once a week from a phone box nearby, which she had to walk to as part of her 'plan'. Very often she would tell me that she could visualise a noose hanging from a nearby tree, which she felt was an option for her or, alternatively, on her way back from the phone-box, she might wait for a bus and throw herself under it. I was frantic until I could ring the house phone 30 minutes later to speak to her husband. Having verbalised her 'demons', Bet would invariably be sitting knitting, watching television or brewing up.

Meanwhile, under the circumstances, Paul had decided to spend the bulk of his time with his father, where he could continue to attend the same school, socialise with his friends and, as often as not, he was round our house. Paul spent weekends and holidays with his mother and, when her husband was later posted to Germany, Paul was happy to fly out there once a month. Bet missed Paul desperately but knew he was happy with the arrangements and sacrificed her own feelings in the interests of her son. Despite being busy, I missed Bet too and looked forward to seeing her monthly and to seeing Rachel when on leave.

Jess gave birth to her daughter, Emma, the following July and I have to admit to being as excited and embarrassing as my mother had been when I had Jess. I was an extremely proud grandma and just as nervous when I cut her umbilical cord – Jess's husband was a little queasy and avoided the 'business end' of the proceedings. By then I had completed my second year and, other than my part-time work, was free to enjoy time with Martin, my children and Emma. Adam and Katy adored Emma, taking turns to feed and hold her on Friday nights when she stayed over. During this summer, Jess and family stayed at our house for two weeks whilst me and Martin were able to go on holiday. This was a wonderful, magical time for me as we had time for each other and, at last, I felt that I didn't have any major worries; life seemed to have taken a turn for the better and I couldn't remember a time when I hadn't been pre-occupied with one crisis or another. Although not achieving particularly well at school, Adam appeared happy and settled, and Katy was embarking on her final year at school, contemplating applying to college for child-care courses.

My final year at university flew past. I had chosen to study developmental psychology, criminology, counselling, mental health, and psychology of women. I continued to soak up information like a sponge and loved to weigh up the pros and cons of theoretical perspectives and practical applications, paying particular attention to issues of discrimination and oppression. Rather than ignore areas that caused me confusion, I would go the extra mile in order to fully understand and remained an avid reader throughout. This meant that, although it was hard work, I had no problem in completing assignments when the time came or in revising for exams. For my final year thesis, I had chosen to do research at a local Social Services family centre, in evaluating response to the Children Act 1989. Although I appreciated the value of statistical information in certain circumstances – I still do – I particularly wanted to examine the experiences of staff and the women they worked with, via a series of semi-structured interviews. I put a lot of effort into this particular endeavour, became a volunteer and ran the 'drop-in', in order to gain the trust of service users, and remained with the project for two years until personal catastrophe struck once more. I was well rewarded for my efforts and missed getting a first by three percent. I was over the moon at the graduation ceremony, which was made special on hearing Martin and my kids cheering me from the balcony.

I decided to take a year out before going on to study social work; I needed a rest and wanted to be around the home and my children more. I had continued to maintain contact with my former employer who had taken over the care of her mother alongside an agency worker. Sophie's condition had deteriorated and she had suffered a further two strokes; her daughter was finding it difficult to manage and was suffering from depression herself, and so I resumed my old duties on a more or less full-time basis. I also had time to get to grips with my own house and spend more time with Martin.

Unbeknown to me at the time, this 'blissful' state was only to last around five months.

Chapter 7

In late autumn of 1992, we had begun to have concerns regarding Bet's son, Paul; he was nearly 16 at the time. Paul had returned some weeks before from a holiday with his father and had not returned to school, taken to staying in bed, and complained of 'vague' ailments, including feeling sick. Bet was in Germany at the time and extremely worried. I reassured her that I would go to see Paul and see what was wrong; it had been three weeks since he had been round and this was very unusual. Paul was tired, uncommunicative and really couldn't be bothered with me. I wondered if he was depressed, having problems at school or just 'swinging the lead'. I persuaded him to visit his G.P. with me, with the promise of a taxi to take us. The G.P. concluded that Paul had gastroenteritis and prescribed appropriately. God forgive me, I didn't know otherwise; I made Paul walk home with me thinking it would do him good.

Within three weeks, on Boxing Day, Paul was subject to emergency admission to a specialist unit, suffering from the advanced stages of heart failure. The whole world came crashing down around the family. Bet returned from Germany to move in with me, my children were in turmoil, and life was pure torture once more.

My employer, bless her, agreed to confirm to the benefits agency that I was working 16 hours a week for her, in order for me to claim benefits; in fact I worked eight hours and she paid me well above the amount stated. Obviously Bet lost her income, whilst her husband struggled to pay his way in Germany, arrange a transfer to England on compassionate grounds, and transport their belongings home. It took four months. In the meantime, I had to support Bet, as she was ineligible for any financial support. Again we attended the hospital, miles away, on a rota basis for the next ten days. Bet practically lived there. Following assessment, Paul was discharged from hospital awaiting a heart transplant and, of course, there were no guarantees.

We had a visit from the transplant social worker who explained the procedures and legalities of the situation. She gave loads of information, encouraged the family to stay positive, and followed it up with the statistics regarding life expectancy should Paul be fortunate enough to receive a donor heart. I left Bet with her ex-husband and went round to a friend's house seeking comfort. How could we be positive? We were all in shock and I was certain that Bet and her husband hadn't really been listening to the hurriedly presented statistics. Up to the last month, Paul had been a seemingly healthy teenager with no history of heart problems and I felt that the options were for him to die now whilst awaiting a heart or die within the next ten years at maximum, aged 26.

On a day-to-day basis, the time was spent caring for Paul in his own home, to allow his dad to continue to work. Bet spent every morning with Paul, whilst I concentrated on Bet and my children's emotional and physical needs, joining her in the afternoons. When Paul's dad came home, Bet would return to our house whilst Katy and Adam would visit Paul. Finances were biting hard due to the multiple loss of earnings and taxi fares to and fro; Martin had recently been laid off work and was finding the search for alternative employment difficult and so was unable to help out. Fortunately, Paul quite quickly received disability benefit, most of which was used to entertain him and tempt him to eat. On days when Paul felt up to it, we would take a trip out; he particularly enjoyed trips to the 'flea market', where he would buy whatever took his fancy. We were fully aware that Paul was living on borrowed time but we dared not go there, concentrating on trying to keep him occupied, amused and comfortable.

Paul had been issued with an emergency bleeper and, thankfully, we did not have to wait long. Much of that night passed in a blur; I can't even remember who looked after the kids. Bet, Paul's dad, Martin and myself waited for nine hours in the relatives' room and no one was available throughout that time to report on progress. I had looked on whilst Bet said farewell to her son prior to going into theatre, trying hard to hold back the tears and stay strong for her. Whilst Paul's heart was being removed in one part of the hospital, ours were being ripped apart in another. I can't recall us talking to each other much; we just sat there like zombies experiencing our own private hell. Bet's husband arrived from Germany and Rachel from the South of England just before Paul came out of theatre. Bet took a room at the hospital for the four weeks up to Paul's discharge, which, although reasonable, put further strain on our collective finances. Paul's transplant took place the day after Valentine's Day, which gave special significance to the hearts and flowers seen in abundance on his 'transplant birthday'.

Having already applied for a place on the DipSW course, my interview was scheduled for the next day. I was on automatic pilot as I attended and completed the written assignment, and the individual and group interviews. I have no idea how I got through this, remaining calm and focused. At the end of the day I was offered a place and set off back to the hospital thinking nothing of it; my mind was elsewhere. Following the transplant, Paul looked fit and healthy and we all concentrated on supporting him in meeting the necessary medical, psychological and practical milestones, crossing one bridge at a time. Paul learned how to manage the cocktail of drugs, which were to keep him alive, and we learned of their complex and wide-ranging side-effects, interactions and contra-indications.

We also began to understand the processes of rejection and infection, which would threaten him for the rest of his short life. I admired Bet for her emotional strength during this period; as one life-threatening situation was negotiated another one loomed large. We all tried to support each other as much as possible, whilst trying to stay sane. This was not without difficulty as we were all in a 'different', sometimes conflicting, emotional state. My children visited often, especially Adam and Katy, who were particularly close to Paul. Jess was less available due to having

Emma, a recent house move, working full-time, and having just discovered that she was pregnant for the second time.

Paul faced the usual post-transplant difficulties, including the frequent hospital visits; during the first month this was on alternate days and gradually became fortnightly. The frequent heart biopsies were painful and distressing to him and for us and, in between the trips to the specialist unit, there were weekly visits to the local hospital for blood tests. Following analysis of blood, one or more of the drugs would need to be adjusted, which meant frequent appointments at the G.P. On one occasion, the G.P. refused to vary the dosage of one of the more expensive anti-rejection drugs, on the basis of the cost to the surgery. Bet and the rest of the family were angry and distraught, having to chase around to secure the support of Paul's consultant in order to challenge the GP. The steroids led to massive weight gain, whilst the anti-rejection drugs caused Paul to become depressed and have stomach-ache. Further drugs were prescribed to combat the side-effects, which also included acne. Like all teenagers, Paul resented having to take his medication, especially when they made him feel unwell, and talked a lot about just wanting to be 'normal'. He had already negotiated the tricky psychological questions regarding whether he would think and feel the same way, now that he had a young girl's heart.

During the summer and autumn of that year there were times when Paul had to be admitted to hospital, as a result of feeling unwell due to infection, rejection, or based on blood test results. This was always a time of high anxiety as we quickly learned that the drugs taken to control rejection of the heart lowered Paul's immune system and left him open to infection.

Conversely, in controlling any infection the anti-rejection medication was reduced, thus increasing the potential for rejection. As such, for most of the time it felt like we were sitting on a ticking time bomb and we were largely helpless.

At the time I took up my place on the DipSW course, things appeared fairly settled; Paul had been offered a place at college to do car mechanics, Katy was on a child-care course and my second grandchild, a beautiful baby boy named Rhys, had been born. I had supported Jess and her husband during the birth and again had the privilege of cutting the cord. Jess was a nightmare whilst in labour this time. Normally so kind and placid, Jess blamed her husband for everything and told me to 'shove the gas and air up your arse, mother', when I tried to help her to manage the pain.

Bet and her husband had been posted to a nearby garrison town and Paul spent much of his time there. Again I studied hard and did well with the coursework; the university had very high academic standards and, when the monthly coursework results were published, there were always a number of people in tears. As a class we were mutually supportive and tried to help each other as much as possible. Some were beyond it! I recall one student in particular who challenged a small group of us to show him the research that proves sexual activity with a child to be harmful, if undertaken within the context of a 'loving relationship'. The scary thing was that he was serious and, at the time, was managing a resource for children. I remember telling him to 'fuck off', reporting him to staff, and I think he was forcibly ejected sometime soon after.

Because of my background in psychology, I was familiar with many of the theoretical perspectives and debates which social work utilises. I was free, therefore, to give my attention to areas I knew little or nothing about; this included legislation, policies and procedures, and specific areas such as disability. I was also keen to extend my knowledge regarding the psychological and socio-economic impact of the various forms of discrimination and oppression. I had long decided that I wanted to specialise in children and families, but remained interested in furthering my knowledge and understanding of other client groups, and the issues that impact upon them. Right from these early days I knew that preventative work was to be my forte. My experiences and, quite frankly, 'who I am' dictates that I am not cut out for the adversarial nature of the courtroom; nor did I want to be. Of course, I have always remained aware that this is an important area of social work and that some people enjoy the challenge. For me, the prospect of writing endless reports and spending much of my time 'paper-shuffling' was not where I wanted to be. Suffice to say, I was never going to be a career woman; I don't have that kind of ambition.

Being realistic, I knew that paperwork is a necessary evil and that the quality of outcomes for families is based on the quality of assessments, the effort put into working together with other agencies and professionals and, most importantly, the face to face relationship with clients; at least in terms of preventative work, although I would argue that this is the case in any area of social work. I also knew that 'policing' families went with the territory. I was blissfully unaware, at that point, of the true nature of the intra-agency political machinations, which conspire against clients and workers alike.

Having said all this, I knew that things weren't going to be easy. How could it be in such a complex line of work! I suppose what I'm trying to say is that I've never subscribed to the 'pie in the sky' notion of social work as all about 'helping people'. I knew I would have to challenge clients in respect of the care and control of their children; I also knew that successful intervention is based on the personal qualities and characteristics of the worker in establishing a working relationship. After all, I had encountered a number of people in 'authority' that I would gladly have shown the door. And so, I completed my first academic year and looked forward to my practice placement. I had also begun taking driving lessons again but, sadly, had three failed tests under my belt and was struggling to pay for the lessons. My placement was in an inner city family centre, which was hours of a job getting to and from. I was only there for a period of two weeks before unavoidable events yet again overtook us.

I had gone to bed early the night before my driving test and was awoken in the early hours as Paul had become unwell. We took him to hospital and were informed that he was experiencing an episode of severe rejection; the severity of rejection and infection was 'measured' according to a numerical scale. The outcome was to hang in the balance over the next few days. I took my driving test because I'd paid for it and there was nothing I could do at the hospital. I passed! I took the rest of the week off from my placement as, once again, life was in a constant state of flux.

I contacted the university to say I needed to abandon the course and explained the circumstances. I can't say I was happy with the decision but felt I could not go on; I couldn't give of myself and retain my commitment whilst my own family needed me. I didn't want to. Thankfully, the head of the department rang me back some days later to suggest I defer until the following year. I set about acquiring a part-time job at another residential home for older people in order to claim family credit, as it was at the time. I had to set aside the unused portion of my grant as, obviously, it would be needed if I managed to continue the next year.

Paul came home from hospital and, during the next year, had more than a few ups and downs. The uncertainty of his condition meant that he was unable to take up the offer from college, and often felt lonely and without focus, despite spending most of his time with his mum, dad and the rest of us. He did have a small number of friends who visited on a regular basis, but Paul continued to yearn for 'normality' and whichever way he looked at it, it remained elusive and out of his reach.

My hours of work at 'Oakdale' were 3pm until 7pm and the odd night shift in order to remain eligible for benefits. Katy was at college at the time and Adam was 15. The hours didn't really fit but I didn't have much choice. It did mean that I could cook tea, during term-time, and be available to Paul during the day if he wasn't staying with his mother. Adam and Katy were quite able to take care of themselves in the early evenings and Paul's dad was around, should they need him, after he finished work. I had only been working for around four weeks when I received a letter from the Council offering an appointment from the rent rebate officer. I hadn't a clue what it was about and arrived at the duly appointed time like a lamb to the slaughter. The official cautioned me, telling me I was the subject of a fraud investigation, and taped the interview. It was an extremely unpleasant experience and I could tell she didn't believe a word I said; moreover, I was treated despicably. I felt humiliated, upset and angry, and it took a further six weeks to sort out. It seems that the Council were under the impression that I was working, claiming benefits and my grant; as it turned out, they ended up owing me fifty quid, but I never received an apology and the stress of this, on top of everything else, took its toll.

At work it soon became clear that all was not as it should be. The home was owned by a local G.P. in partnership with a consultant gerontologist who, given his line of work, should have known all about the care of elderly residents. Much of the necessary equipment was antiquated and downright bloody useless, and staffing levels were poor. The 'matron' was hardworking and 'creative' in meeting the needs of the residents; unfortunately, this was usually at the expense of staff that were poorly paid and their caring nature exploited. Staff regularly contributed to the 'amenities fund' intended to provide residents with social activities and other 'extras'; it was later discovered that the owners, aided and abetted by the matron, were using these funds to buy footstools and soft furnishings, and to pay for internal decoration.

Food cupboards and the fridge were kept under lock and key and ingredients for meals fastidiously calculated. God forbid! If you dropped an egg then someone had to do without! As there were only ever two members of staff on shift at any one time and were therefore unable to leave the building, key-workers were obliged to undertake residents' personal shopping on their own time. There were also a number of residents who were fairly mobile and staff would take them out for a walk either before or after their shifts, otherwise they would never have gone anywhere.

Residents had to be in bed by 9.30p.m., whether they wanted to or not, otherwise the 'routine' became unmanageable in the mornings with only one member of staff on duty. Lydia, aged 85, was one of the more physically able residents and in possession of all her faculties. She used to cry when made to go to bed early. On the nights I worked, I refused to make Lydia go to bed and we watched *Carry On* films together late at night, whilst I did the ironing. I would take her something in for supper and she enjoyed the company, as she was unable to converse with many of the other residents. Lydia liked to stay in bed awhile in the mornings and at the age of 85, why shouldn't she? Of course, I got into a great deal of trouble for allowing this as, when my shift ended at 7.30am, it was expected that all the residents should be up and dressed. This meant starting at 5.30am and I was advised, by the matron, to start with 'Ida' who was blind and would therefore be none the wiser.

Staff morale was extremely low and no one seemed to care. The week before Christmas I discovered that 'matron' had deducted one hour's pay from each worker's wages, to buy paperweights for the 'doctors'. Other workers told me that this was always the case but that the doctors never reciprocated. I challenged the matron on this and many other issues and was promptly given the sack. The staff team got together and we sent letters to the owners outlining grievances and requesting a response. The owners set up a meeting on my last day, when I was escorted from the premises and not allowed to attend. Staff made it clear that I had voiced collective opinions and that, if they did not reinstate me, they would withdraw their labour. I wished they hadn't done that, since they all received their 'cards' the following Monday and the home ran on agency workers for the next six months before the owners decided to sell. Most of the women found work fairly quickly, but I still felt bad because many were single parents or their families had very low incomes, whereas I knew that I would be returning to university.

I found work as a cleaner at a nearby factory for the next few weeks, in order to remain eligible for benefits. I'd been in contact with the university for some time and been offered a placement at a local probation office. The week before I was due to start, Paul was admitted to hospital for the final time; he was having difficulty passing urine and it was discovered that he was suffering from multiple organ failure. I can't even begin to find words to express how I felt nor how I knew others to be feeling, especially Bet and Paul's dad. Again we assembled at the hospital, where we all spent the day, and were eventually told his condition was stable. We returned home for some rest and were awoken during the night and called into the hospital. Bet was physically sick. Paul had been taken into theatre for some surgical procedure or other; the details of that night and the following day remain vague to this day.

We were told several times during the next 24 hours that Paul would be unlikely to recover, only to be told within the next hour that each 'crisis' had been averted; we were also told that the extent of brain damage could not be assessed whilst he was under sedation. This was an emotional rollercoaster, which threatened our collective sanity, and we hardly dared hope. I remember thinking of Paul's desire for normality as his survival once again hung in the balance. Eventually, Paul was transferred to the High Dependency Unit and we were told his struggles were coming to an end. I watched whilst Bet cradled her beautiful baby boy in her arms, as he died, aged 18.

Life came to a standstill for the whole family. During the next fortnight no one went to work, college or school. We spent most of the time together grieving and supporting each other, staying up late and only falling asleep when sheer exhaustion took over. Since Paul had died the day before Valentine's Day, two days short of the prescribed two years post-transplant, the family were told there would need to be a post-mortem. This was to prove an equally harrowing time as it again raked over the circumstances of Paul's death, along with the re-opening of raw emotional scars. Katy, Adam and Paul's friends from the youth club chose two of Paul's favourite tracks to be played at the funeral, whilst I contacted school to explain Adam's absence. In the event, school rang to enquire why Adam was still absent, as we were awaiting arrival of the hearse on the day of the funeral. We said our public goodbyes as 'No Woman, No Cry' and 'Don't Worry, Be Happy' was played at the crematorium during a non-religious ceremony; our private goodbye was negotiated the week after, when we buried Paul's ashes at our local church so that he could be near to home.

Rachel had, by now, finished her time in the Navy and had bought a house in Cornwall. Bet's husband had engineered early release from the Army on compassionate grounds and the two of them joined Rachel. Bet needed to get away for her own sanity and we all desperately needed some semblance of normality. Bet suffered terribly and, up to this day, remains prey to night-time 'terrors' in the form of dreams of Paul's final minutes. In an effort to avoid the questions and stirring up distressing emotions, Bet would tell people she hadn't got any children, whenever she was asked. It took a long time to encourage Bet not to deny her son's existence in this way, because it was clear that doing so hurt her terribly. Similarly, I had to discourage Rachel from shifting Paul's photographs in an attempt to 'save' Bet from being upset. We all suffered, one way or another – especially Adam.

Adam, aged 16, entered a sort of 'wilderness' in which he had to wrestle with the question of his own mortality; he began to display all kinds of concerns and worries relating to his own physical health, and became quite anxious and depressed. Adam was convinced that there was something wrong with him and, up until the last three years (aged 25), would avoid mention of Paul and his granddad. Adam refused to return to school and found a job at the local factory. His mind was never on his work and he made lots of mistakes and attracted the attention of 'factory bullies'. On one occasion, he was grabbed by a group of lads, through a car window, and dragged several yards by the throat at speed. Adam's father went to the factory but, by now, it was too late and Adam would not return. Over the next few months, Adam tried his hand at various 'casual' jobs but found he couldn't stick with anything. A visit to the G.P. proved less than useless as she 'interrogated' Adam and her aggressive approach closed him down further. We did manage to get him to see a counsellor but he was not ready to negotiate the depths of his emotions; instead, he was prescribed anti-depressant medication.

Adam's recovery was to be a long haul and the worst was yet to come.

Chapter 8

I didn't have time to miss my sisters too much, although I was conscious of the fact that I missed their physical presence. By the time I took up my placement at the probation office, both my sisters had found work in Cornwall, as had my brother-in-law. Rachel planned to take Bet to America to try to give her some positive focus; the three of them then set about the business of day-to-day life whilst I threw myself into my placement, in between worrying about and supporting Adam. Martin had, by now, got a mortgage and had moved from his mother's into a house of his own. It meant that he was less able to subsidise my household, though he tried to do what he could. He had, several times, asked me to marry him, but I knew that the financial burden would be too much and likely to destroy the relationship; Katy and Adam were still at home, dependent upon me, and I had another 18 months at university.

I worked hard whilst on placement, enjoyed learning new things and, being a student, I had time to spend with clients. I quite enjoyed writing pre-sentence reports but was less enthusiastic about attending court to 'speak to' such reports. I hated the court etiquette, the rituals and the adversarial nature of the courtroom. I can recall being so nervous, on one occasion, when the Probation Officer had to leave the court room, leaving me alone. Thankfully, the defence solicitor bailed me out but could do nothing to intervene when, bowing to the magistrates on leaving the court, I got so flustered I tripped over my skirt and fell full-length through the double doors into the corridor. How embarrassing is that? Whilst most of my work was with adults, I did have the opportunity to work with a number of young offenders. What motivated me was the preventative work I was able to plan and engage in, with individuals on probation and supervision orders.

Many of my clients were poor and had multi-faceted difficulties to deal with. I recall one young man who had been rejected by his mother at the age of 15 and had 'dossed' around with friends, getting himself into trouble with the police from an early age. His mother had had alcohol problems of a long-standing nature and, from what Barry had told me, the family had an extremely chaotic lifestyle. When I first met him, Barry was passively uncooperative. His 'crimes', and he had a string of them, were all of the stupid variety; he had various convictions for theft which, in total, probably amounted to a thousand pounds, and he had spent several months in a young offenders' institute. Barry had a skewed view of relationships, both on a personal level and with those in 'authority'. I felt fortunate to have the time to build a relationship with Barry and in attempting to promote his understanding that life doesn't have to be like this.

By the end of the placement Barry had got himself an agency job, his own flat, had packed in his habit of drinking a litre of cheap cider a day, and was going swimming every day instead. Barry understood the concept of 'guilt by association' regarding his choice of friends, however unjust it may be, and was beginning to think through the consequences of his actions for others and, most importantly, himself. I would love to be able to claim the credit for this but, quite simply, Barry achieved this for himself. What I can say is that the working relationship we were able to establish acted as the catalyst and, within the constraints of my position, I always met him on 'equal ground'. Barry once told me that he couldn't believe I was a 'probation officer', albeit in training, because I was so 'normal'. I took it as a compliment.

The probation office held 'gate-keeping' meetings on a weekly basis, whereby a selection of court reports could be read by colleagues when the writer was dealing with issues such as disability, culture, gender or sexuality. This was intended as a forum for discussion and to help eradicate the use of unhelpful stereotypes. One of my reports was forwarded by my practice teacher on the basis of its potentially stereotypical nature. The client concerned was a mother of three and had admitted to DSS fraud. In giving a full picture to the court, I felt it was necessary to outline her caring responsibilities towards her children and her ailing mother, in addition to societal expectations of her as she herself perceived them. On the basis of the interviews I had had with her, it was clear that these issues were major contributory and mitigating factors which needed to be worked on once she was sentenced. With hindsight, I realised that my practice teacher had intended this to be an opportunity to evidence competency. I don't think either of us was ready for the slating I got from others who just didn't get it; in their view, stereotypes were discriminatory and to be avoided at all cost, even if it reflected the reality of people's lives.

Whilst I worked hard, I passed my placement without difficulty, despite one or two 'cock-ups'. One of which, I recall, was during a home visit to an elderly man who was repeatedly involved in handling stolen goods. Following his latest conviction, Sidney had been reporting to me for some weeks and, although he was known to have problems with alcohol, there was no mention of drugs on file. I arrived at his flat by public transport and set about helping him to organise his calendar, so that he wouldn't miss important appointments; Sidney's health was not good and his memory was worse. In the middle of this, Sidney sat down and openly applied a tourniquet to his upper arm and proceeded to attempt to inject. Innocently, I told Sidney I had no idea he was diabetic. He laughed. After another attempt he said, 'Fuck it, I'll neck it', and emptied the contents down his throat. I left fairly quickly, laughing at my own naïveté. Sidney continued to visit the office, though I didn't visit him at home; he looked smart in his worn pin-striped suit and always reminded me of Albert Steptoe. On his 76th birthday Sidney asked me to marry him. It took all my powers of self-control to be able to thank him for the compliment and let him down gently.

About halfway through the placement my next grant cheque failed to arrive; I had been doing okay up until now, with more than a little help from Martin. Martin had paid for my books and bought me a computer; up until now my assignments had to be done at home in longhand and I'd had to travel to the university to type them up. Ironically, I was listening to 'hard luck' stories from clients who assumed I might be an 'easy touch'; if only they'd known I was in a worse position than them! As the weeks passed I had frequent contact from the rent office as I had fallen badly in arrears. I had just as frequent contact with the grants office, never speaking to the same person twice nor getting any understanding of the position I was in. It got to the point where an eviction notice had been served on me and the housing department were baying for blood.

The grants office were telling me the cheque had been dispatched eight weeks ago and housing were saying nothing could be done unless I provided written proof of when I could pay; of course, the grants office couldn't do this. I spent every lunchtime using the 'firm's' phone to try to sort this mess out. I even contacted the university, with little success. Martin had been buying food for us but, having to pay his own mortgage, was unable to do much more. I struggled to find the kids' dinner money and bus fares to my placement. Eventually, one of the senior Probation Officers offered to lend me £300. Thankfully, the original cheque was cancelled and re-issued, so I did not have to borrow any money. Towards the end of my placement I received a telephone call to say I had an uncollected cheque which they had discovered down the back of a filing cabinet.

My practice teacher gave me a glowing report and stated that I was capable of much more. I was a bit bemused at this comment as I felt I had given my all and hadn't a clue what she meant. On my last day, she drew me aside and told me she'd noticed that I always sat on the same side of the desk as my clients when working with them; she asked whether I had felt comfortable with this and whether I thought her clients might feel she was stand-offish, as she preferred to have the desk between them. I didn't know what to say. The way I was with clients had come naturally to me and was more 'common sense' than training. Of course, in the case of the unknown or where there were safety issues or angry/aggressive clients this was different. To be truthful, I couldn't understand why an experienced worker and practice teacher needed to ask such a basic question. Another thing that made me laugh was that right at the beginning of the placement she had enquired about my family. On learning that I had grown-up children and grandchildren, she was satisfied that I had a 'support network'. Herself single and with no children, she was blissfully unaware that I was their support network and not vice versa. Obviously, this was something she was required to establish as a practice teacher, regardless of the lack of any real understanding. I still see her occasionally; she now has two teenage children, has benefited from the experience, and has a far more realistic view of life.

At this point, Martin found employment in Germany, having been laid off once more; the engineering business being either famine or feast, he was continually changing jobs accordingly. Adam had remained quite depressed and unmotivated, though still saw a few friends, whilst Katy swapped her interest in childcare for a career in sales and had moved into her own flat. I found work for the summer in another residential home for older people which, although it did have its problems, was nothing like Oakdale. The remainder of my time was spent around the house with Adam, continuing to support and motivate him, which was not without difficulty. I managed to see Martin about once every six to eight weeks when he returned home, and I went to stay with him once or twice during the next 18 months he was in Germany.

When I returned to the university in September, it was to join an already established class; the group I had started with had graduated in June and I felt like a fish out of water. I soon settled but it wasn't the same and I was glad when I started my final placement. Money wasn't so much of an issue – it never is unless you haven't got any! With Martin earning decent wages and saving some money, if I was short I could use his spare cash card. After saying this, I didn't go daft, but I did get the back door re-glazed after all these years and managed to take my son to play snooker on a regular basis. My placement was with children and families on a 'front-line' duty team which served an area of high unemployment, deprivation and social problems. I took to it like the proverbial duck to water, enjoying the new learning experiences and opportunities it afforded.

On my first day I 'shadowed' the duty social worker, who was taking office appointments. As I recall, there were two of them – duty A and B; duty A did office appointments in the morning and took duty phone calls in the afternoon, whilst duty B did the opposite. Anyway, some of the office appointments were with potential clients requesting help or members of the public expressing concerns; others were parents/carers who had been invited in to discuss concerns which had been brought to the attention of the department. On the second day I asked if I

113

could cover duty, which was well received by 'duty A' as it meant he could get on with his own work, whilst being available to me if needed. I continued to cover duty on two days per week throughout the placement and thoroughly enjoyed the variety. I also carried a small caseload but, at this stage, being a student I was unable to be involved with child protection investigations, or to hold cases where children were on the child protection register.

My first visit on this placement was memorable in a number of ways. I was told that this case was held by 'the team', as I accompanied another worker en route to the house. The child was aged five and was well looked after by her maternal grandmother, whilst her mother was serving a two-year sentence in prison. The difficulty was that grandma, granddad and uncle tended to indulge in binge drinking every so often, as a family, and when this occurred they would contact the office to arrange care for the child from an aunt. It had apparently taken some time and effort from the team to get the family to comply, but was worth it in terms of the child being able to remain with the family and the cost to the department should she need to be 'Looked After' by the Local Authority. We arrived at the house and were greeted by grandma, who was apparently suffering from some degree of brain damage, as a result of being hit over the head with an iron by granddad during a previous drunken brawl. Gran had a fresh bruise on her forehead and a trickle of blood was visible under her broken glasses. Granddad looked more like Rab. C. Nesbitt than Rab. C. himself, lying on the settee in his string vest and smelly socks. The uncle had a large fresh gash on his cheek, with bits of toilet paper stuck to it.

You couldn't have put a pin between the empty cans and bottles stacked up on the large 'long john' coffee table and the three of them were completely arseholed; it was 10.30am on a Monday morning. The granddad moved his feet and, patting the stinking place they had occupied, invited me to sit down. I perched on the arm of the chair instead. It took us two hours to get the information we needed and to get out of the house, during which time we were subjected to singsongs and a trip around the family album. The uncle enquired whether I had any children, following this up with, 'Come here and I'll give you another one'. Once we had finally managed to make the necessary arrangements for the child we made for the door. My colleague asked when gran thought the session would end and was told, 'about a week on Wednesday'!

One of the earliest cases I was allocated was to support a teenage mum. I was later told by my practice teacher that she thought, at the time, that this would be a good one for a student! It turned out, as is often the case, that scratching below the surface of seemingly straightforward cases often reveals a can of worms. Visits to the family revealed an extremely chaotic lifestyle where access to the house and, by default, the children within, was openly extended to anyone who wished to take advantage. I left the house one day as it was going dark and headed for the bus stop. I was unnerved by a man who came out of a house three doors down and who seemed to be taking an almost menacing interest in me. I saw him again on my next visit, as he watched me from his window. He followed me to the bus stop when I came out of the house. He made the hairs stand up on the back of my neck and I just knew he was trying to stop me from visiting the house by frightening me.

I found out this man's name, from the family, and discovered that he was known to the department. He had a conviction for sexual assault and had not received a custodial sentence on condition that he agreed to an in-patient psychiatric assessment. Later reports stated that he had been released into the community after he tried to set fire to the psychiatrist on the ward. Eventually, the younger sister (age 11) disclosed to me that this man had raped her twice. The child was interviewed by the police, the details of which were harrowing, and the man was arrested, charged and released on bail. I became concerned because the man was living with a woman who had three young daughters and discussed this with my practice teacher. I was told there was no mechanism for 'internal' referrals and, on my practice teacher's advice, I rang the police. And so it was that I, acting as duty A at the time, spoke to the policeman I had reported the crime to initially. The policeman, at my request, duly rang us back to make a referral to duty B who was sitting opposite me.

As my placement came to an end I had very mixed feelings, due to the fact that I had enjoyed it so much. I was particularly pleased with my practice teacher's comments both officially and 'off the record'. She told me that there had been much discussion in the office, as the general consensus was that I was 'too good' to be a student and she had thought I may be 'a plant'. It made me laugh, as I certainly hadn't felt I was 'too good'. During the final phases of the placement I had begun to research and interview individuals and families (including my own) regarding the psycho-social impact of heart transplantation. At the time, little research had been undertaken and what there had been was of the statistical variety. As such, I plodded through research journals which reported seemingly nonsensical conclusions on post-transplant 'quality of life' based on measures such as how often patients went to the pictures or out for a meal. Underneath all the spiel and statistics, I wasn't so sure that what they were actually 'measuring' was quality of life.

What was most noticeable by its absence was the subjective account of the transplant recipient and his or her family. Since, at that time, there was no further time (or funding) allotted to complete research, I had to find work to keep us going whilst I continued. At the same time, I was invited by the Heart Transplant Unit to collect statistics for their ongoing research, in return for access to families as part of my own research. I began to work part-time for an agency contracted to provide home-care for elderly people and people with a disability. The pay was poor but I figured that it would give me the time and energy to concentrate on finishing my interviews and my Masters degree. I had also saved some money from my grant in order to supplement my income. In the event, what with the demands of the hospital, work and Adam, any academic progress was slow and extremely hard.

By this time, Adam was 17 and registered as unemployed; he was increasingly socially isolated from his peers and often presented as confused, anxious and perplexed by the most basic of life's day to day demands. I used to take Adam to the job centre on alternate Wednesdays; otherwise he would never have got there. He was still low in mood and the anti-depressants seemed to have little effect; he spent much of the day in bed and resisted any attempts to help him. In the evenings, Adam would venture out with me to visit his sister; he felt 'safe' under the cover of darkness. Adam was well on the way to developing a social phobia and I felt powerless to help him; he felt sure that there was something 'wrong' with his brain and no matter what I tried it was like pulling teeth.

I enjoyed working with people in their own homes, although the time allotted was never enough. My 'round' consisted mainly of weekend working, helping people to get up, dressed and breakfasted, and visiting later at tea-time and/or at bedtime. I remember the frustrations of having 20 to 30 minutes with each person and knowing that, more than anything else, human contact and interaction was what clients desired most. Of course, this was never 'factored in' when assessing needs. I recall an elderly woman whom I visited who rarely had contact with her family. Ada was quite depressed and had a number of medical and mobility problems. She used to like me to have a brew and a chat with her rather than make her tea and then 'cut and run', and would talk of her youth and life experiences. I would often take longer than my 'contracted' hours to complete the round, collecting prescriptions, running errands or chatting.

On one occasion I found Ada on her hands and knees, praying for the Lord to 'take her'; she had rung her daughter to ask her to visit and been told she would visit a week on Sunday as usual. I spent more than my allotted time that morning sitting and talking to Ada; what was the point of forcing her into her clothes and sitting her in a chair with her breakfast? Ada was distraught and sobbing. I left Ada warm and comfortable in her dressing-gown with a brew and some biscuits, telling her I would be back at tea-time. For this I received an official warning from the agency.

Occasionally I had to rendezvous with another worker from the agency, as it would take two of us to attend to some clients' personal needs. At 8pm one cold winter's night I drove to a nearby town for my regular visit to Bob. The other girl was apparently new, and was late and unfamiliar with the area, but nothing fazed Bob. He had initially introduced himself as an 'ex circus dwarf'; he was a fascinating and amusing individual who had many stories to tell and had worked all over the world with a number of celebrities. Unfortunately, Bob had an accident which had resulted in the loss of his lower limbs and, hence, his need for assistance. Whilst waiting for the other worker, I made Bob's supper and sat looking at his many photo albums. As time went on we decided to get on with the bedtime routine in her absence. I helped Bob to have a wash and get undressed; Bob preferred to sleep 'in the raw' as pyjamas restricted his movements and irritated him. Bob seemed to think we could manage between us, in getting him out of his wheelchair and into bed – which we did in a fashion.

And so it was that I found myself pinned to the bed face up, by a stark-bollock-naked 'circus dwarf'. Obviously, all of Bob's weight was contained in his upper body and head, and neither him nor me could move. We lay there laughing for about ten minutes and, as the laughter subsided, Bob enquired, 'Do you come here often'? Following it up with, 'It's bloody marvellous what you can get on the National Health these days'. At this point the other worker arrived and also began to laugh

119

uncontrollably. She was unable to assist for at least five minutes as she stood in the doorway with her legs crossed and literally peed herself laughing. I was very late for my next call, which seemed to take forever. On my way home, at midnight, I took a wrong turn and ended up going the wrong way up a one-way street in the town centre. The police pulled me over and informed me that my back lights weren't working either. That was the straw that broke the camel's back and I ended up blubbering incoherently about a naked circus dwarf, needing to get home, and the fact that I'd only earned £5.50 all evening. I guess the poor copper took pity on this miserable wretch and offered to drive behind me all the way home.

Shortly after this, Martin returned from Germany. Of course, I was pleased to see him and to spend time with him but this placed extra strain on my time. I appealed to the university for extra time to complete the research and was given a further 18 months. I decided that now was the time to look around for a 'proper job' but I was aware it wouldn't be easy. Obviously I wanted a qualified post but it had to allow for 'hands on' preventative work with families. I continued to work for the agency up to the point where my services were no longer needed and I registered myself as unemployed. Disappointed by the lack of preventative initiatives I successfully applied and interviewed for a position in a Local Authority children's home, subject to a satisfactory police check. I decided that this would be the best move at this time as I had no previous experience of this client group and felt it to be a missing part of the jigsaw. It took five months from interview to starting work, which wasn't what I expected; however, during this time me and Adam had moved in with Martin and we set a date for the wedding.

Due to the fact that I had not worked full-time for a number of years and had spent the last six years at university, I had not made any N.I. contributions and was therefore ineligible for benefits. I was called into the job centre for an interview to 'help me to find work'. I explained that I already had a job but was awaiting police clearance. I eventually spoke to the manager, who informed me that unless I had a start date I would have to agree to 'widen' my choice of jobs, since I hadn't had much luck in my chosen area. I tried to reason with him and showed him the letter of appointment. It met with little success, so I told him to put me down for bricklaying and ballet dancing and left pretty quickly; after all, I hadn't lost much except the N.I. stamp which was all I was receiving.

Martin and I were married in May that year; we used to joke that we'd had a longer engagement than Ken Dodd. It was a small, inexpensive affair, culminating in a four-day 'funnymoon' in the Lake District. Immediate family and friends gathered to wave from outside the pub as bride and groom departed on the back of a Honda Gold-wing. Unfortunately, neither of my sisters was there as both had work commitments and couldn't afford the trip. Rachel was, by now, working in a Young Offenders' Institute and Bet was working for the NAAFI in Cornwall. Bet had found some comfort in being around young servicemen away from home who were around the same age as Paul. Naturally, if they were experiencing difficulties, Bet could be relied on to help, advise and assist.

On my return from honeymoon, I found a letter stating that I could take up my new position in two weeks time.

Chapter 9

I spent the next two years working in a children's residential setting. The pay was not great as my qualifications were not recognised and my designation was as a worker, as opposed to that of an officer, though there was little difference in the nature of the work. I did interview for an officer's post a while later, but was told I did not have the necessary two years' experience of looking after and working with children and young people, to which I objected fairly vocally.

I encountered Naomi (aged 14) on my first shift, when she had returned from a drunken spree and held the broken neck of a glass bottle to my throat. I later learned that Naomi could be charming and cooperative, but that she was also severely damaged and disturbed. Naomi had been removed from her birth family as a result of physical abuse and neglect at the age of five, along with her older and baby sisters; they had been adopted quite quickly by a couple who, I understand, wanted to adopt a baby and agreed to take all the girls in order to do so. Naomi was returned to 'care' at the age of nine, along with her older sister; apparently the baby was 'perfect' and no trouble at all. Quite recently I've heard that we are involved with 'baby' now that she is herself a teenager and her behaviour is less than 'perfect'. Due to the lack of foster carers, Naomi had originally been placed out of area, eventually ending up in a private residential home where it was subsequently discovered that she had been sexually abused by a member of staff. Following further moves, Naomi went to a private placement in the same area with a one to one staffing ratio; she was now sufficiently emotionally damaged for individual foster carers to be unable to cope with her challenging behaviours. Naomi built up some positive relationships with her familiar caregivers over the next three years until the department decreed that she should return, along with other young people in 'out of area' placements.

For many of the young people, this was the right move as they had not only 'lost' their families but also friends, community and sense of self; it also made sound 'business' sense, since out of area placements are incredibly expensive and place great strain on resources we don't have. In Naomi's case it was disastrous as she was rejected and abandoned yet again. By the time she came to us, Naomi was not about to let anyone in. Naomi would only ever go so far and would then instigate a 'fall out' when she felt anyone was getting too close. She was unable to trust anyone or to risk emotional involvement for fear of the pain separation would bring. It was all she'd ever known. Naomi was ultimately abused more by the system than she had been by her birth family. The problem, as I saw it, was a product of 'blanket' money-saving policies without regard to individual needs and circumstances. Frequent changes of social worker meant that Naomi's 'history' was consistently overlooked and there was no one to challenge the decision, which reinforced and amplified the damage. Naomi's behaviours eventually became too much for us to cope with, in the context of the needs of the other young people, and she was moved on somewhere else.

In a recent training event, I raised such issues in earnest. As with most of these types of 'training', it was intended as an awareness raising exercise. Young people who had experienced the care system had been invited to address the audience of mainly social workers and support workers, in order to tell their stories. I can understand its value with regard to inexperienced workers and to give these young people a voice but, due to the number of factors which outweigh the control the social worker has over his/her cases, it masks the real 'culprit', so to speak, and reinforces the illusion that such matters are within the control of the individual worker. Does anyone ever consider how mind-numbingly frustrating it is to participate in such events; to be told what you already know and see on a daily basis; to be held and hold yourself accountable, yet know you are completely and utterly powerless to intervene? Still, it helps the training department to dispose of their budget according to the latest research findings and legislation, and functions only to fulfil the requirement to evidence meeting performance indicators, which are totally out of touch with the realities of practice. But, forgive me, I digress.

My research suffered as a consequence of the fact that I was more interested in meeting the needs of the children than I was in academia. I learned a great deal from my time in residential, most of which reinforced my desire to engage in preventative work. I learned of the difficulties of dealing with challenging behaviours but, unlike parents, I was able to go home at the end of my shift. I also saw the damage caused to children and young people as a result of being rejected by their families. Whilst academic knowledge promotes understanding of the issues, there's nothing as powerful as seeing it first hand on a day-to-day basis. These kids can end up so screwed up for the rest of their lives unless they are fortunate enough for someone to be able to reach them in time, or to have stable placements with caring, 'switched on' foster carers. Obviously, there will always be some situations where children need to be removed from abusive parents, but there are many other cases where preventative work would have averted this need.

Like Naomi, many of the young people had been subjected to multiple moves and the subsequent impact of fractured relationships and instability, which compounded their difficulties. Understandably, the children and young people regarded staff as 'paid to do a job' and therefore uncaring; I tried very hard to do whatever I could to reach them, often coming in on days off to take one or the other to a school play or community event. Most of the young people displayed challenging, aggressive and often violent and destructive behaviours, which was extremely draining at times. I never had any problems with any of them when with them on 'my own time' and neither did other staff members. Outside of these times, the young people were increasingly institutionalised, engaging in 'us and them' behaviours which often led to night-time riots.

Many a night, staff would be held 'hostage' on the landing with young people refusing to go to bed, disturbing other kids and, on one occasion, firing coat hangers and bits of wood from bedroom furniture at staff. This meant that the following morning I was often dragging myself around 'half-dead' whilst the kids caught up on their sleep. I found it hard being unable to intervene because it was obvious that the kids did it 'because they could'. Similarly, with Naomi we knew that when she went out she would consume alcohol and drugs, and engage in sexual activity; all we could do was to advise and hand out condoms – even though we knew that there were adult males waiting nearby to exploit her.

As in society in general – though it may be seen as controversial to say so – the young people were given more rights and freedoms than they were/are mature enough to exercise. In my opinion, that is the function of parents and carers. Often the knee-jerk reactions of well-meaning but misplaced political correctness backfires on the people it is intended to protect. In Naomi's case, her social worker colluded, stupidly, with Naomi's stated desire to become a model and instructed her key worker to take her to a model agency in London. Thankfully, her worker managed to sabotage this plan. Naomi was not 'conventionally' attractive and it would have destroyed her self-esteem to be rejected. Again, it's down to interpretation, as young people's wishes and feelings should always be taken into account but not necessarily acted upon.

Social workers rarely visited. Now I understand why; they simply don't have the time and, when prioritising cases, they know that Accommodated children are (mostly) safe in comparison with those in the community. This also has its downside because they don't have a relationship with the child and often don't understand why they do what they do. Naomi, for example, rang her social worker to make a complaint about me at 1p.m. one day. She had returned in the early hours and disclosed she had taken drugs and felt unwell. I had spent the night with her in the A&E department at the local hospital, returning at 7a.m. I had one hour's sleep before being on duty again, was feeling worse for wear and was not my usual self, though I did try. I woke Naomi at 12.30pm and took her a glass of water and tablets for her headache. Naomi obviously noticed I was tired and immediately took offence. Although she was damaged and largely unable to see beyond her own emotional pain I had a fairly good relationship with Naomi. I also knew that Naomi would look for rejection whether it was there or not; it was almost 'hard-wired' in her brain and Naomi's best form of emotional defence was attack.

When Naomi's social worker arrived, she was very matter-of-fact. I understood the need to investigate the complaint, but she was cold and rushed in her approach to both of us and didn't seem to see that Naomi was over-emotional, distressed and needing comforting. The worker continued to question Naomi, ignoring the tears, for around half an hour. I couldn't stand it any longer and put my arms around her, whereupon she dissolved into great wracking sobs and hugged me back. The social worker grunted, picked up her briefcase and rushed off without so much as a by-your-leave. She really didn't know Naomi and the fact that she didn't acknowledge I'd been on duty since 2p.m. the day before really pissed me off.

The 'waking night' supervision was executed on a rota basis. After the first few months there were difficulties as most of the staff were refusing to do it and some had left as a result. I offered to work nights, three days a week for the next six months, until new staff members were in post. I felt that this would give me the chance to complete my research during any settled periods when other work had been done. Albeit my working week now only consisted of three shifts and the same pay, I was hopeless at working nights. I never felt awake day or night and, of the four rest days, it took three days for me to adjust and feel 'normal', by which time I was returning to work. If it was quiet during the night I would try to read and make notes but was always in danger of falling asleep. I took to leafing through magazines and saved chores until around three a.m. which was always the worst time for me. I can safely say that I'm not a natural night worker.

The internal décor of the establishment left a lot to be desired and, I was told, there were no funds available to rectify this sad state of affairs. The Manager turned out to be a very creative accountant and I found a way of keeping myself awake during the night. It cost very little to make the place 'child-friendly' and homely. Each of the young people chose colours and fabrics for their rooms, staying in the spare room in turn, whilst I decorated their bedrooms during the night. Having done this, I went on to re-decorate the kitchen, dining-room and lounge. I must admit to feeling more than a little dismayed when I later discovered that the Authority sold off these premises to a private residential initiative, whilst retaining a similar property down the road which was not in such a good state.

During this time Katy gave up her flat nearby and moved to Newcastle to further her career in sales. What with my concerns over Adam and niggling worries about Katy on her own in Newcastle, I was glad to return to day-shifts and to re-enter the world of the living. Shortly afterwards I successfully re-interviewed for an 'officer' position and abandoned the research entirely. Me being me, more practical tasks and interests took precedence and I convinced myself that I didn't need a Master's degree to be a good social worker, which was all I really wanted. What drove me was the fact that something was bound to turn up and, in the meantime, I had plenty of time and energy to spend with Martin and Adam and to visit Katy and my sisters.

By the age of 18 Adam had been spending more and more time with his father, who was still living around the corner from us. I had very mixed feelings about this as James had retired from the Fire Brigade, on the basis of emotional ill-health disguised as 'back problems'. Having commuted his pension from the Navy, James had received a large lump sum from the Fire Brigade with which he proceeded to fund his drinking. I was glad for Adam to at last have a decent relationship with his father but concerned that James now had a drinking partner – Adam. I tried to talk to James to no avail and he and Adam began to go out regularly together, returning very late and in a stupor. I realised that both James and Adam were 'self-medicating' with alcohol and it allowed both to escape their difficulties whilst under the influence. The alcohol compounded Adam's problems and he would often come home and spend the night crying, ranting and raving or otherwise disrupting the household.

Thankfully, this did not last long, as it was clear that Adam was unable to handle the alcohol, which was screwing him up more. No matter how hard I tried, Adam refused to address any of his issues and further convinced himself that the way he felt, when sober, was evidence of some physiological defect in his brain. Fuelled and propped up by the alcohol, Adam felt able to be 'himself' and to go out and socialise. As a result, he was often ejected from the local pub and got himself into trouble with the police on two occasions through sheer stupidity. He found that he felt much more at home in his own skin after a few bevvies and began to believe that the more he drank the better he'd feel; unfortunately, he never suffered from hangovers. After not having seen his dad for a few days, Adam was told by his uncle that James was in hospital. I took the kids to see their dad and we were told that James had been admitted with alcohol-related medical problems, had been critically ill, and that it had taken three days to find out who he was. James was later told that his next drink could be his last and he resolved to abstain.

Adam moved to live with his father shortly after James was discharged from hospital. James kept to his promise regarding alcohol and seemed better able to manage Adam. Now sober, James was able to talk to Adam 'man-to-man' and Adam responded positively. James took a part-time driving job and swapped his obsession with alcohol for playing bingo when he finished work. Sometimes he would pick Adam up to accompany him or, depending on my shifts, I would drive Adam to meet him for a game of snooker. Although he still had his problems, Adam was much happier at his dad's; he was able to have a bigger bedroom and to use one of the other rooms to play snooker. Obviously he was unable to drink as much since his father was no longer paying but, when he did, he often caused havoc; he would come around late at night wanting to talk, oblivious to the fact that I needed to get up early for work the next day.

I became more and more concerned over Adam's mental health, as he began to have periods where he seemed totally divorced from reality; he began to express some fairly bizarre thoughts and feelings which he hung onto in the face of all evidence to the contrary. He was admitted into hospital one afternoon following consultation with the G.P. Adam was not making any sense at all and was extremely distressed when I got him to the surgery; he did not object to staying on the psychiatric ward due to his confusion and the fact that he was frightened. I contacted James, who agreed to visit that afternoon whilst I went to work, having arranged with the ward staff to visit when I'd finished my shift. I'm not sure how I managed to work that day, but I was relieved that Adam was safe and may now get the help he needed. James rang me to say that Adam discharged himself during James' visit and was now at home. I was relieved to see that Adam was now coherent but unable to explain what had happened to him; much later he admitted to having taken a mixture of 'speed', 'dope' and alcohol the night before, given to him by the 'mate' he was out with. He has never, to my knowledge, taken anything since.

I took some leave from work at this time and took Adam to Cornwall to stay with my sisters. Adam was reluctant to go and spent much of the time in bed, though he did take the dogs for a walk and went to the pub one evening with my brother-in-law. Martin was unable to take time off work but came with us for the weekend, returning two weeks later to pick us up. Adam did benefit from the peace and quiet and, Lord knows, I was glad of the support from my sisters. During the months to come, Adam's condition deteriorated, and he took to staying in his room at his dad's and would rarely engage with anyone. I was frantic! On occasion Adam would say he thought he heard voices but was unable to distinguish what was said. He agreed to see a psychiatrist, who was quick to diagnose Adam as schizophrenic. I knew full well what this meant but hoped that the anti-psychotic medication would stabilise him; at the same time I worried that Adam may be one of the 20 per cent or so for whom medication has little if any impact.

Adam's diagnosis meant frequent trips to the G.P for repeat prescriptions and medical checks. This became an organisational nightmare, as the G.P wouldn't prescribe unless he saw Adam and Adam wouldn't leave the house. I would organise these appointments on my days off and for late afternoons; trying to explain this to the doctor or receptionist was guaranteed to produce blank looks. It would take me most of the day to encourage and cajole Adam to keep his appointments. Sometimes it worked and sometimes it didn't, and there was never any way of knowing which it would be. Adam's medication was reviewed on a monthly basis and, for whatever reason, the G.P. refused to review them collectively (he was taking four different types), which meant I had to go through this rigmarole on a weekly basis. If I was unable to get Adam to the surgery, he didn't get the tablets. I did try to enlist the help of the psychiatrist but there was nothing he could do. Additionally, Adam suffered from many disturbing side-effects and felt little benefit. Of course, this meant that I had a hell of a job getting him to take them.

Although there was no doubt that Adam experienced some psychotic symptoms, I was unsure whether or not his diagnosis was correct. My sisters and Martin were convinced it wasn't, but I knew this to be a complex disorder which can take time to fully develop. I wanted to believe that the psychiatrist had got it wrong; quite frankly, I wanted to bury my head in the sand in the hope it would all go away. It didn't. They say that what doesn't kill you makes you strong. I didn't feel so strong and I was fed up of the struggle. It seemed to me that whatever I did it was three steps forward and two back. In fact I was feeling sorry for myself and, once again, I feared for Adam's future.

Visits to the psychiatrist were an education, illuminating in more ways than one. Psychiatrists 'rotated' on a six-monthly basis and Adam attended every three months. This meant that, if he was lucky, he would get to see the same one twice, although this was rare. In those days I worried that I may be viewed as over-protective – the typical 'schizophrenogenic' mother; he certainly had the stereotypical 'inadequate' father. Nevertheless, I always went in with Adam and we always went through the same palaver. Largely speaking, the psychiatrist had not looked at the file and the first 15 minutes were usually spent in silence whilst s/he perused the documents therein. These appointments could be confusing for Adam; they certainly were for me at times, which was another reason I went in with him.

On the one occasion we saw the same person twice, I came out of the office feeling very confused and I didn't have a mental health problem! Dr Longthorn had asked about medication and I gave him the names and dosage of the drugs Adam was taking. He seemed quite perturbed at one of them and began flicking furiously through the file; he was a sight to behold with his pants at 'half-mast' and the full cuff of his sleeve visible under his too-tightly fitting jacket. As he scratched his head with his pen, Dr Longthorn demanded to know how long Adam had been taking this medication and who had prescribed it, as there was no record on file. When told he had, the last time we were there, Dr Longthorn cleared his throat, told Adam to discontinue the medication and scribbled something on his file. That was it, no explanation, nothing.

There was no one for Adam to talk to or to alleviate his fears. I tried to encourage Adam to carry on 'as normal', because what else could we do? I recall one rather unhelpful conversation with a neighbour, who 'advised' me to let him get on with it as I'd done my best and it was likely that Adam would now turn to violent crime, because that's what schizophrenics do; I didn't know whether to laugh or cry at this obviously highly educated statement. Nevertheless, Adam continued to retreat into the safety of his own room and we spent hours and days there together. In an effort to capitalise on the times when he felt okay, I took him to play snooker after finishing my shift or to the supermarkets late at night when they were empty, so he could choose videos to watch during the day. These outings were largely unplanned, due to the fact that Adam's moods were unpredictable; this meant that I was often totally knackered by the time I fell into bed. Martin tried to be supportive but he struggled to understand and deal with Adam in the early days, whilst working 12 hour night shifts. As time went on we settled into a kind of routine and, whilst Adam grappled with his many anxieties, his condition didn't get any worse. We managed.

On the work front, things were looking up. I had spotted a job vacancy within the Local Authority I was working. I knew I wanted that job and was hell-bent on getting it. The vacancy was for a qualified family support social worker within an intensive support team. The team had evolved from a residential setting, its main aim being to prevent family breakdown and subsequent reception of children and young people into care. Each worker carried a small caseload, which often comprised chaotic 'dysfunctional' families with multiple needs. The team was available to service users seven days a week for up to sixteen hours a day. This meant that there was always someone available to respond to crises across the team's full caseload. There were also a small number of residential beds available within the building for times when it was not possible to resolve conflict that night and workers would return with the child the following day to continue negotiation. The team comprised qualified social workers and experienced residential workers, some of whom had counselling qualifications.

This was the job I was looking for. Whilst working in a residential setting, I had seen a number of crisis admissions and young people languishing in care, with few attempts made to re-unite the family and not a social worker in sight. I was so excited at the prospect of working with this team. The unsocial hours and sleep-ins didn't bother me in the slightest; the pay was good and the ethos of the team was fantastic. I interviewed for the job and didn't put a foot wrong. With hindsight, I realise I didn't have to try to work out what they were looking for because I was 'it'. I answered honestly and enthusiastically; I really couldn't contain my excitement about the innovative work of this team and was upfront regarding my genuine desire to be part of it. Having said that, I really didn't know if I would be successful and my nerves 'kicked in' when I returned home. I had been told that I would be informed of the outcome by 6pm that night, and I was so excited and nervous that I didn't know what to do with myself. I got the job but was more than a little tipsy by the time I found out, due to the fact that I'd needed a couple of whiskies to calm my nerves. Much later I confessed as much to the deputy manager who'd rung me; she laughed and told me she thought I'd sounded 'over-excited' or pissed.

My departure from residential coincided with preparations for Davy to return home to live with his mother. Davy was a darling, though he could also be a handful and, due to his size and strength, could be very challenging and intimidating. Davy had a learning disability with emotional behavioural difficulties and was desperate for the love and attention of his mother. Davy had been removed from his family at an early age due to the incestuous relationships therein; his mother had aided, abetted and participated in such activities and Davy had been passed around family and friends for the same purpose. Over the years, Davy had been re-educated regarding appropriate physical contact and it was now felt that it was safe for him to return home. Davy had been awarded a sizeable sum of money via the courts, which was held in trust for him until now, when he reached the age of 16; apart from a small sum he had earmarked to redecorate his room and buy a music system, Davy intended to give the rest of his compensation fund to his mother. I've often wondered how life turned out for Davy; I guess he must be 30 or so now.

Anyway, I couldn't wait to share my good news with my family and I arranged a celebratory meal. It meant so much to me to be able, at last, to do the work I had dreamed of and the extra money would make a difference to all our lives.

I wasn't disappointed as the job turned out to be all that I wanted, and more.

Chapter 10

I started work with great gusto. This team was a hybrid version of intensive family support and more 'traditional' case-holding social work, with the added bonus of residential facilities. Team members needed to have extensive experience of children and families, including work in a residential setting. High maintenance families, in terms of the complexity of issues, family dynamics, and amount of support needed, were the 'bread-and butter' of the team which I had now joined.

Because of the way in which this team was organised and run, it was possible to take a holistic and flexible approach to the work. As the team was increasingly receiving referrals for the type of support offered, in respect of child protection cases, this obviously warranted employing more qualified workers to hold these cases, which was where I came in. All team members had a working knowledge of colleagues' caseloads and were updated during weekly team meetings. Families were introduced to all members of staff during the period of involvement and most responded well to workers who attended when called out in a crisis.

Families who had previously received a lengthy period of traditional social work involvement tended to fare particularly well under this system, due to the time and attention workers were able to give. The quality of service was excellent, even though I say so myself. As such, workers were able to help remove some of the physical, psychological and societal barriers to progress, the key to which was contained within the working relationship itself. Being the case-holder and the worker, it was possible to keep track of, and respond appropriately to, the ever-changing circumstances which presented, whilst retaining focus on the child and the purpose of intervention.

Basically, we knew our families well and there were very few who didn't respond to the service on offer; we would always begin with building relationships with family members to gain their trust, working on the issues which they identified as a priority, so long as the children were 'safe'. More often than not parental issues, both current and historical, hold the key to improving the care and control of the children. At the risk of stating the obvious, people generally need to feel that you listen to and understand them in order for them to trust you. There's no doubt that it's a difficult balance between remaining 'professional' and being approachable and empathic towards parents/carers; after all, I wouldn't 'bare my soul' to someone I didn't trust, would you?

I never had a problem with revealing personal aspects of your own life if I felt it would help, so long as you don't overburden people who have enough difficulties of their own; of course, you'd be daft to give out information that could be used against you at a later date. That's why it's important in this job to have worked through your own baggage and potential prejudices (we all have them), otherwise any cracks are bound to catch you out or you're likely to project them onto others, coming to the wrong conclusions, doing people a disservice and not making a difference at all. The one thing I've always tried to do is see things from the other person's perspective; after all, we all have our own story to tell. Like I said, it's a difficult balance but it is, more often than not, achievable – it just takes time and for the worker to be themselves. For some of the adults (and the young people for that matter) the very fact that someone takes an interest and shows they care can produce a placebo effect.

Of course, there are occasions when all you're doing is flogging a dead horse and you need to recognise this in order to prevent yourself becoming embroiled in the family's chaos. I 'inherited' one such case from another worker, following her retirement. I knew all about the family due to the fact that the department had worked with all of the children at some time or another and at least two of them had spent time 'in care', having been abandoned. The mother was apparently fine with babies and continued to produce a large number of them; when each child reached the age of around 11, it was chaos. I'd been introduced to the family by the worker (Ruby), who I'd known for a number of years. Ruby told me that 'dad' was a lorry driver who worked three nights a week, was always on a short fuse, and kept a shotgun behind his chair which he would brandish about if anyone pissed him off.

I visited the family often and, although there was little change, managed to convince them that I wasn't taking Ginny anywhere. In the early days crises occurred daily but it was always possible to negotiate a truce. On one visit I could hardly keep my face straight as dad got himself into such a state I thought he'd have a heart attack. I can't remember what his daughter had done but Alf was almost apoplectic. Just as I thought we were getting somewhere, Ginny swore at him; Alf grabbed a stepladder, which was resting at the side of his chair, and chased her round the room threatening to 'knock her fucking block off'. After separating the two of them, Alf shouted, 'See, it's the swearing I can't be fucking doing with. She's an ungrateful little bastard'. Ginny sat sniggering in a corner.

We never found out where their money was coming from; the whole family were dripping in gold, had nice clothes, a lovely home and very expensive holidays. I discovered they were going away at the same time as me this year; same day, same flight, same destination. I didn't know what to do, since this holiday had been planned for some time and my sister, Bet, was coming up from Cornwall with her husband to join me and Martin. This was to be a holiday of a lifetime. I'd never been anywhere 'exotic' before and it was just too complicated to change the arrangements now. Meanwhile, my manager congratulated me on 'a fine piece of community social work', supporting my clients whilst on holiday. I didn't find it funny! In the event, 'mum' had got the dates mixed up and travelled the following week. Thank God I saw neither hair nor hide of them and thoroughly enjoyed the holiday.

On this team methods of working were creative, innovative and proactive, being tailored to the needs of family members. At its most basic, there was no point banging on about what the adults should and should not be doing in respect of care and control of their children, in the absence of identifying and working with the source of resistance to change. This was the case with 'Mr Ice Pick-Man', so named because he had presented at the benefits office with an ice-pick with which he proceeded to threaten staff; he had also pitched up at school threatening to hang the teacher and warning her to watch her back. Undoubtedly, Steve was an angry man; his stepson, John, was at risk of physical abuse and his name had been added to the Child Protection Register, following an injury he received at the hands of his step-dad. Steve and his wife (John's mum) were heavy drinkers and Steve later admitted to his addiction but unfortunately refused help to address it. In response to the harsh treatment he received at home, his parents' drinking and the influence of peers, John was rebelling big style.

Initially, visits to the home were undertaken in twos, because of the risks involved. After a short while it became clear that this was not necessary and that Steve's aggressive 'bark' was worse than his 'bite'. Alongside the work I was doing with John and the family work with all three, I spent time with Steve at the family home in order to fully engage him in the plan. Believe me, it wasn't easy and Steve would take exception to everything said and done. We began to discuss his childhood and I encouraged him to make links to his experiences, how he had dealt with them and the person he had become. Over the coming weeks I learned of his own upbringing, littered with violence and fear, and how he responded in turn with violence, intimidation and rebellion against anyone in 'authority'.

Steve had worshipped his mother, who had her own difficulties and had suffered from anxiety and depression. Steve learned to fight for his own survival in his early years and had continued to do so in the face of evidence to suggest this approach wasn't working. As a teenager, Steve had been sent to a 'Borstal-type' establishment from which he graduated to being a young offender, followed by periods as an adult prisoner. When faced with any difficulties, Steve only knew one way to respond – with his fists. Steve cried like a baby when talking of his mother and how the whole family blamed him for killing her, following her death from a deliberate overdose. Steve was 14 and locked up at the time.

I tried to encourage Steve to see the benefits of 'brain over brawn' and gradually he came to trust me. Steve's intention was to stop John from leading the life he himself had engaged in and he began to realise that all he had been doing was training John to be just like him. At the end of our involvement, Steve told me that no-one had ever treated him with any respect except me and that he could honestly say that I had never pissed him off. He laughed when I told him that there were numerous occasions when he had pissed me off, which was true. The upshot of this piece of work was that John could remain with his family, although the situation remained far from ideal; it also represented huge savings to the department as a result of averting the need for foster care. John was one of the young people who had a regular respite 'slot' with us on nights where I was the 'duty worker' for the team and sleeping in.

John called in to see me some years later, having spotted my car parked outside the 'new' building I later worked from. He was 21 at the time and, although life could not be described as perfect for him, he had his own flat, a job, and had managed to preserve a fairly positive relationship with his mother. Unfortunately, his step-dad had developed alcohol-related health problems and had died quite recently. Steve had continued to ring me for about a year after the case had closed and, although he did accept and act on information regarding counselling, sadly he ran out of time concerning the alcohol addiction.

I was well aware that, on other social work teams, workers did not have the luxury of spending time with service users, which was why I'd held out for the 'right' position. In recent years this situation has become much worse, as I later learned to my peril. The beliefs, values and ways of 'being' with clients utilised by the team, in addition to the teamwork, which was essential, were clearly visible in relationships with colleagues. After all, social work theories and methods of working relating to the 'human condition' are useless if not applied to workers themselves. The work could be draining at times, but colleagues were always supportive and readily available should there be a need to 'offload'. Management adhered to the same principles as workers, in terms of supportive and collaborative ways of working, both with service users and within the team. In short, values and beliefs were an integral part of the work and not simply regurgitated at interviews, or other public events, and then locked away in a cupboard until the next time. For me, this was quite effortless as it was the way I tried to live my life. At the same time, I have to say I'm not Teflon-coated; I swear and smoke like a trooper. I also get frustrated and angry and drop the odd bollock here and there.

Generally speaking, we were a happy bunch and invested greatly in meeting the needs of the children, young people and their families with whom we worked. I used to sing on my way to work, though thank God no-one could hear my tuneless renditions! I've not done that for a long while. Nevertheless, workers were always happy to go that extra mile, often turning up to meetings when not on shift or staying late to support colleagues. We were also flexible regarding shift patterns and changes, including covering each other's work. It was extremely hard work but the rewards were great and the system ran like clockwork.

On a personal level, colleagues and management were aware of my difficulties with Adam, as I was aware of their personal circumstances. This meant that if I needed time off at short notice, others would volunteer to meet pre-arranged commitments. Unfortunately, workers from the mental health team who were working with Adam were not afforded the same luxury. In the seven years of involvement, Adam had 13 different support workers with gaps of weeks, sometimes months between. Some of them left to gain qualifications but most, I suspect, got fed up and just left. For Adam, this was catastrophic as work never really got off the ground; as each new worker came on the scene we were back to square one, and Adam lost confidence and interest over a period of time. Adam really only got a service due to his schizophrenia 'label' and the need to 'monitor' obviously took precedence over the work. Initially, there had been family sessions with myself and Martin but I was never fully sure of the objective, especially as each session was taped for 'training purposes' and we weren't offered a copy, nor received feedback; suffice to say it was all a bit mystifying and, however well-intentioned, I'm not sure they really knew what they were doing.

Adam was duly introduced to his new worker, Judy, and we discussed plans to help him to address his social difficulties. Judy was commissioned to encourage Adam to challenge his 'paranoid' thoughts and feelings regarding other people looking at him and talking about him. Although I felt that Adam would have responded better to a male worker, he got on well with Judy; it would have been difficult not to as she was a really nice person. The time came for Adam to try to 'test out' his progress, and Judy arranged to pick him up and go out for an hour. I returned from work to find Adam agitated and upset and now more convinced than ever that people really were looking at him. Unfortunately, Judy had thought fit to accompany Adam to the local Conservative Club at lunchtime; Adam had never been seen in the company of a young woman before and of course had attracted much attention and gossip. Moreover, the tiny village we live in was exclusively white at the time (it still is) and Judy is of Afro-Caribbean ethnicity. The villagers had a field day and for quite a while afterwards people would 'casually' enquire as to who Judy was.

The plan had backfired badly and had actually made Adam worse; instead of alleviating his anxiety and 'proving' to himself that no-one was paying any attention, Adam found that everyone was staring at him. I spoke to Adam's community psychiatric nurse to try to rescue the situation. Unfortunately, she misconstrued what I was saying and looked at me as if I'd taken leave of my senses. I tried to tell her that neither Adam nor I were racist and that the plan could have worked if Judy had taken him to a nearby town, where no-one knew him, but that it was doomed from the start in the village. The CPN looked at me blankly and in a way I can only describe as passively hostile, as she offered me a complaints leaflet; I declined. The damage had already been done. As with my experience at the gate-keeping meeting within Probation, issues regarding race and other areas of potential discrimination can provoke a knee-jerk reaction which suspends common sense. It was another 18 months before Adam was willing to try again. In the meantime, I continued to support Adam as much as I could, in addition to my daughters. The fact that I was happy at work and in my relationship helped me in responding appropriately to Adam and in feeling optimistic about the future.

Martin continued to work nights and, because of my shifts, I was often around during the day, so we got to spend time together and to go away for the odd weekend. We also got lots of opportunities to get together with Adam, the girls and my grandchildren, who frequently stayed overnight at weekends if I wasn't working. My grandchildren were growing fast, aged around seven and four; Jess and her husband were both working hard and me and Adam visited often at the end of my shift, depending on how he was feeling at the time. Katy returned from Newcastle, still working in sales for the same company, and was living in a flat quite close by. If I wasn't consoling her as a result of having been dumped by the latest boyfriend, I was consoling the latest boyfriend because she'd dumped him. She certainly kept me busy. Bet and her husband continued to share Rachel's house in Cornwall and the three of them seemed fairly settled. Of course, Bet never fully recovered from Paul's death, and continued to struggle with life without him and with the prospect of knowing she would never have grandchildren of her own; life would never be the same for her but she dealt with it the very best way she could.

Bet became a volunteer fund-raiser for the Cornish Heart Foundation, along with her husband, and was leading a fairly busy life. On Paul's birthday that year, as always, we lit candles in his memory and spoke to each other on the phone. On Mother's Day, my children always buy flowers for 'Auntie Bet' on Paul's behalf, and Bet planted a rose bush named 'Paul's Scarlet' in her garden, which she has taken with her on subsequent house moves. The name of the rose held particular significance because Paul's hair turned from blonde to red, almost overnight, as a result of the post-transplant drugs he was taking. We all managed to see each other on a regular basis but could never quite co-ordinate everyone being in the same place at the same time.

Around this time, I began to work with Barbara and her 15-year-old son. Alex was an extremely intelligent young man who was doing exceptionally well at school and was earmarked for a great future. Alex's projected exam results were phenomenal and he was hailed by his teachers as a potential genius; conversely, his relationships at home and his emotional state were appalling. Alex had been taken to the family G.P by his mother when school had informed her that he had been discovered attempting to cut his wrists with a razor blade. Alex was refusing to see or speak to anyone regarding his difficulties and, understandably, his mother was fraught with anxiety.

Over the next six weeks, I concentrated on befriending Alex and learned of the problems he was experiencing at home. He didn't get on particularly well with his step-dad, for a number of reasons, and had an extremely ambiguous and volatile relationship with his mother. I later learned that Barbara had had an impoverished upbringing, but the family were now enjoying a fairly luxurious lifestyle, thanks to her husband's income and the fact that she worked seven nights a week in a residential home for older people. Barbara was house-proud to the point of being obsessive, hardly got any sleep, and was essentially meeting herself coming back; stress levels within the household were unbearably high and you could cut the atmosphere with a knife. I always had to take off my shoes before entering the house, as did anyone else, and Barbara would watch me like a hawk wherever I sat and kept removing, plumping up and replacing the cushion behind me.

Alex wasn't allowed to go out, due to his mother's fears regarding what other young people were up to and her well-intentioned but unnecessary directive that her son should spend all of his time studying. Rows would erupt at the least provocation and both of the adults seemed to twist things around so that it was always Alex who became the scapegoat; even when the rows were between Barbara and her husband (Gerry), Alex would cop for it from both sides and with both barrels. Work with Alex and Gerry was easy, in comparison to working with Barbara, and the two of them began to get along a little better quite quickly. Gerry agreed that Alex needed to be allowed to go out and mix with his peers but Barbara was having none of it. She did, however, agree to me liaising with school so that Alex could sign up for after-school classes, on the basis that he would be supervised and 'learning' something. Fortunately, most of the clubs he joined were as much for pleasure as business, but neither me, nor school were about to tell Barbara. It was a start.

Alex started to grow in confidence and made a few decent friends. At this point things seemed to be going fairly well and I was considering closing the case; Alex had not self-harmed for a number of weeks, seemed much more up-beat, and even his mother appeared a bit more relaxed. Soon after, following response to a crisis call from the family late one evening, the situation took a turn for the worse. Barbara had discovered that Alex had struck up a relationship with a young girl he met at the after-school club and had stopped him from going. Barbara was in a total frenzy and was adamant that Alex either live by her rules or he had to leave; it took two hours to persuade her that she and her husband should go to bed whilst Alex stayed with us overnight.

Alex started to self-harm within two days and also took an overdose. He agreed to see the hospital psychiatrist, providing I accompanied him and his mother. I knew that it was Barbara that needed the help rather than Alex but to get her to see this was almost impossible. By this time Alex was also pulling his hair out in clumps and hadn't attended school for two weeks. As we were crossing the car park, Barbara spotted a young white-coated doctor and began a verbal assault on her son; she screamed to him that he (Alex) could probably achieve the same status, if only he would listen to her. Alex was pulling his hair out at the time.

Eventually Barbara began to open up and talk of her own feelings of failure at not having achieved much academically. We began to unpick this slowly and Barbara acknowledged the source of her anxiety which she was projecting onto her son. By the time the case closed things were much better. Barbara was attending counselling herself and was slowly coming to terms with the fact that she could not live her life through Alex and could advise, support and guide, but not control him.

Alongside families needing to make changes in order to remain together, there were many others who perceived the answer to their problems to be simple; they wished to abdicate parental responsibility and put their children 'into care'. Whilst sympathising with such individuals and offering to support them, it was made clear that the Authority did not look after other people's children. In reality, if they were determined enough and refused all efforts to engage them in effecting change, we had no alternative. In Kirsty's case this is exactly what happened.

Kirsty was 14, not attending school and constantly arguing with her mother. I began to work with (or should I say not with?) the family, following an emergency referral when Kirsty's mother had rung to say she'd thrown her out. When I arrived at the house Kirsty was sitting on the doorstep, along with four black bin bags containing her belongings. Aside from these were her school uniform, books, music system and other associated items, which were strewn the length and breadth of the street. It was a cold winter's evening, lashing it down with rain, and no matter how much I banged on the door and called out, Kirsty's mother refused to open the door. After spending the next half-hour collecting up Kirsty's possessions, much to the amusement of the neighbours, we returned to the unit where Kirsty stayed for the night with me. As it was my 'duty', I was thankful to get into my dressing-gown and shove all our clothes in the drier.

Over the next three days I visited the family home frequently in order to negotiate a way forward. Kirsty's mother (Jean) never allowed me over the doorstep and was completely closed down to any suggestions made. As far as Jean was concerned, the care of her daughter was now up to us. I placed Kirsty with a foster carer some ten miles away and continued to try to work towards returning her home. Jean talked of the antics of her 'wayward' daughter and told me that the last straw had been when Kirsty had stolen some jewellery from the house. Kirsty's response was that her mother had nicked it in the first place and Jean shrieked that 'that wasn't the point'. Kirsty told me that her mother was 'on the game', which Jean didn't deny; according to the family files, both of Kirsty's older brothers and her step-dad were currently detained at 'Her Majesty's Pleasure', for their part in various thefts and robberies.

I contacted Kirsty's birth father, who wasn't interested due to the fact he had remarried and had a young family with his new wife, including two of her children from a previous relationship. Meanwhile, Jean informed me that she was planning a house move and was refusing to divulge her new address or contact details. In desperation I eventually got to the point where I told her that, in the event of Kirsty's death, the foster carer would need to contact her. The response was that, in that case, it would be pointless. The impact on Kirsty was disastrous and it was about two years before she saw her mum again. I wasn't involved during this time as the case was then transferred to another team, but I saw Kirsty quite recently; she now has two children and is involved with the department in a child protection capacity. I hear that she has mental health problems, had hooked up with a succession of undesirable partners, and experienced domestic violence at the hands of one or two of them. Thankfully, once it was established that Accommodation wasn't an option, in most cases we could work together to find ways of making things 'better'.

Generally speaking, some parents have reached the stage whereby they are receptive to change, while some remain quite fragile; others have no intention of changing and a small minority are downright dangerous. In the case of Lorraine, who occupied both of the latter categories, there were times when I was at my wits' end. Lorraine had four children, all of whom were registered for neglect and emotional abuse. Lorraine had been diagnosed as having a personality disorder and suffered from bouts of anxiety and depression; she was clever and articulate, but a nightmare to work with. One of the children was quite poorly and subject to serial hospitalisation but a definitive diagnosis remained elusive. It was thought that Tanya may have a complex psychological disorder which functioned to put some space between herself and her mother, when the strain of whatever was going on in the household became too much to bear. Alternatively, it was thought that Tanya may be the victim of Munchausen's Syndrome by proxy, or Fabricated and Induced Illness, as it is now known.

Lorraine wouldn't allow any of her children to stay overnight with us and only 'just about' complied with child protection requirements that the children needed to be seen alone. All of the children were very guarded and said nothing without eye contact with their mother, which seemed to direct what they said and to whom. I would take the kids out together and separately, in an effort to engage them; I never got very far because the kids seemed almost scripted and had obviously been well-rehearsed before they came. I always got the impression that they wanted to tell me something, particularly the younger two, but everything they said and did seemed to be very carefully considered.

Provided I steered away from discussing the situation at home or anything to do with their mother it was okay and it was nice to see them smile and have fun; something I never saw them do at home. Jack, aged ten, did once confide that he would like to go to the school bonfire but his mother wouldn't allow him. He gave permission for me to talk to his mum, which I did extremely sensitively. Lorraine said she would take him herself and thanked me for 'being a friend to Jack'. She said it was good for him to have someone to talk to and she appreciated the feedback. The next time I was alone with Jack he burst into tears, saying it was no good and that having me around made things worse, but he wouldn't elaborate; after this, Jack hardly engaged with me at all and looked sad for much of the time.

The children weren't attending school regularly and were at home doing chores and generally keeping their mother company. Initially, in liaison with the school, I concentrated on trying to motivate the kids and Lorraine to improve attendance and to get Lorraine to address the problem of head lice, which was pretty bad. I also tried to befriend her and give her lots of encouragement to use her intellect productively. Unfortunately, Lorraine's personality disorder manifested itself in an ideal of perfectionism that no-one, including herself, could ever match up to; consequently Lorraine seemed to create chaos wherever she went and led me a right merry dance. Lorraine revelled in the attention she got as a result of having a 'sick' child and seemed to delight in 'playing games' with the professionals involved.

At 10p.m. one evening, Lorraine rang me to tell me she had killed the children, laughing manically as she went into detail regarding how each one had died. She played funereal music down the phone, interspersed with cackling, whilst I hung on, heart in mouth. A later visit revealed that all the children were well and enjoying the 'prank' played by their mother. I held this case for about two years and we never got to the bottom of anything. I continued to work on the assumption that if I gave Lorraine loads of time and attention in her own right, perhaps she'd give the kids a break. I'm not sure whether it worked or not, but Tanya's frequent need for hospitalisation seemed to diminish and the family eventually moved out of the area.

At this point I had a good mixture of cases which certainly kept me on my toes. As a rule, the 11-16 year olds were the ones most in danger of being thrown out by their parents who, for a variety of reasons, were unable/unwilling to 'grow' with their youngsters. Some of these parents' expectations were too high, as in the case of Alex, while others had neglected their children's needs when young or their own issues took precedence. In this case the kids had started to fend for themselves, to some extent, and their emotional confusion was reflected in their behaviours. I also had a number of cases of the child protection variety which invariably involve the same factors but have reached the criteria of neglect or abuse of some form. Either way, for change to take place the nature of support offered was the same. The presence of a stable supportive adult, in both child and parent's lives, was crucial in determining outcomes and much of our time was spent in trying to help heal family rifts. In the interim, staff took on this role, decreasing the intensiveness of support accordingly. We didn't have too many 'failures'.

According to the old adage, 'if it ain't broke, don't fix it'. According to the new 'business' framework of current thinking 'if it ain't broke, replicate it cheaper'. Where the cuts are made at grass roots level, generally speaking you get what you pay for and then spend more on senior management salaries to make further cuts and 'manage' the mess you create.

We were just about to experience this process first hand.

Chapter 11

The building we worked out of was originally two three-bedroom houses which had been converted into one and was owned by the Local Authority. It suited our needs perfectly, combining office space in one part and the residential 'unit' in another. We had a waking night-watch person who also undertook 'housekeeping' responsibilities in much the same way as I had whilst working in a residential setting. There were a number of rooms in which family work could take place or, in a crisis, where we could separate family members to work towards resolution before re-uniting and transporting home. It was therefore a great disappointment when we were informed that we would soon be co-located with another team, as the Authority intended to sell. This meant that we lost the residential element and many of the family rooms; it was a backward step, as far as we were concerned, that made our job more difficult and, ultimately, increased the number of emergency admissions into care. The building itself was later demolished and the land was sold for private development.

Looking back, this was the first of many changes to come – and not for the better either! In the new building, there were many practical obstacles to overcome and a change in working practices. We now worked between 8am and 10pm, Monday to Friday. This was usually arranged on the basis of a late shift followed by an early shift, in an effort to maintain some consistency. When undertaking the 'duty' role, the worker would remain on call until midnight for telephone response. Most service users found this helpful and crises could often be temporarily resolved via telephone advice and counselling. As the duty worker would be at work at 8am, s/he could then follow up and do whatever was needed. Weekend work consisted of a 10a.m.-6p.m. shift, with telephone response up to 10p.m. It left a number of gaps in the service and now meant there was no service on bank holidays.

When workers were making visits in the evenings the building was 'unmanned'; this meant that it took extra time to secure and unlock the premises, as individual rooms within were alarmed, which could be as frequent as three or four times a night. The problem of availability to clients was resolved by diverting the phone to the duty mobile and, if necessary, the duty worker would contact a colleague if a crisis visit was needed. It slowed us down considerably, but we could see the benefits in terms of savings made by the department, whilst retaining the 'bones' of the service.

In the early days, two members of the team had developed an anger management programme for young people which we ran on Tuesday evenings. This was a great success and the groups continued to run on a six-weekly rolling programme. At the same time, the 'mums' group had proved to be popular and was productive in a number of ways. It only took two members of staff to facilitate the group and, apart from parenting advice, relaxation exercises, etc. it was used to signpost clients to other services they may need and monitor 'from a distance' how things seemed to be going in respect of child protection cases. Because it was delivered in an informal setting, it also helped to maintain relationships with some of the more 'difficult' customers, and promoted co-operative and supportive relationships between otherwise very isolated women. These were the first things to go.

In preparation for one of the staff meetings, the manager asked us to consider ways in which we could engage fathers and stepfathers in the parenting of their children. When we got to the 'health and safety' item on the agenda, the manager reported concerns that Norm (one of the handymen) had been spotted mowing the lawn wearing trainers; unfortunately, he'd run the mower over the front of his feet, barely missing his toes. I suggested that maybe we could offer DIY sessions with Norm as a way of engaging dads and step-dads. It went down like a lead balloon but a few of us thought it was funny.

We were always short of foster carers (and still are); let's face it the demands and responsibilities are huge and the pay isn't that great. There are many fantastic carers around the borough but more than a few who are a downright disgrace and I had the misfortune of attempting to work with one of the latter. Julie was an ex-prison officer who had largely worked with young offenders; she had many practical skills to share, like playing and teaching the kids to cook and take care of themselves, and she could be extremely patient. On the other hand, Julie seemed to have absolutely no idea of kids' emotional needs, especially when dealing with damaged children. She once told me that it was her job to teach children to behave themselves.

I was working with a single parent of two at the time and needed an emergency short-term placement for the youngest, a boy named Liam, aged ten. His sister (aged 14) acted as carer for her mother who had severe long-standing mental health problems. The sister was supported via the 'young carers' and seemed to have a good grasp of her mother's difficulties and the maturity to deal with the excesses of her mother's behaviours, in ways that minimised the damage to herself. Liam was another story; his behaviour was becoming increasingly difficult, putting more pressure on his sister as a result. Liam was also attempting to hang himself whenever the opportunity presented, with whatever form of ligature he could lay his hands on, and was emotionally 'all over the place'.

I introduced Liam to Julie and all went well for the first couple of days. The plan was to provide Liam with a stable environment whilst I worked with him and his family to address the issues. Obviously, it was important for Liam to retain contact with his mum and sister, but Julie saw this as unnecessary interference and wouldn't co-operate, and so it took more of my time to facilitate contact myself. I rang Julie's support worker from the fostering department and arranged a joint visit in an effort to resolve the situation. This meeting degenerated into a general slanging match and free-for-all (on Julie's part), despite my attempts to approach the situation sensitively. At the outset,

161

Julie told me that she'd met my kind before, that I was a pen-pusher and knew nothing about life. She was extremely hostile and dismissive of anything I had to say, to the point of bawling at me to shut up every time I opened my mouth.

I always spent time with foster carers to ensure that they knew as much as possible about the child they would be caring for and what the child needed from them. In Julie's case, she argued about everything and refused any advice or guidance. To be honest, it was much harder work than dealing with the family and much of the time I could've swung for her. One of Julie's 'rules' was that Liam should take a shower every day and he was refusing; she had threatened him that she would get her husband to drag him and hold him in the shower if he didn't comply. Julie also stated her belief that Liam's attempts to hang himself were for attention – these attempts were increasing as Liam's emotional state was deteriorating – and that his mother's mental health problems were 'an excuse'. Julie went on to regale me with her views that mental health problems were 'non-existent' and declared that she was of the 'spare the rod, spoil the child' brigade.

I tried to get another placement for Liam but there were none to be had. On the advice of the fostering department, me and Julie's support worker embarked on joint sessions to 'bring Julie up to speed'. It was a complete and utter waste of bloody time and, being unable to say what I really needed to say, I just wanted to knock her out. I used to try to remain calm on the outside but I doubt if I fooled her. Inside I was a seething ball of anger and frustration and had a knot inside my stomach every time I visited. She was 'allegedly' a professional, but I didn't see why the department was continuing to employ her; I knew that she was damaging Liam further and passing him off as a 'naughty boy'. How the hell she got through the training I'll never know. I wrote a two-page letter of complaint but it didn't make any difference; I received a letter requiring me to evidence, in writing, every incident as it happened so that they could address it with Julie. I groaned, knowing this meant extra work for me that I didn't have time to complete and just felt that Julie might've been great with some kids, but didn't have the skills or understanding to care for someone like Liam. I also felt that Julie's demeanour was totally unprofessional, but that's another story. Thankfully, the fostering department soon got pissed off with me and found an alternative placement for Liam. Julie began to look after two fairly well-adjusted sisters whose mother had a long-term illness and, I understand, made a good job of it.

I still sang on my journeys to and from work; I believed passionately in what I was doing and what it was possible to achieve. As time went on, more and more work came our way, due to the volume of work coming to the 'front door' of the main social work offices. Those of us who were qualified at the time were now working exclusively with child protection cases, whilst the unqualified workers continued to work with clients on a 'voluntary' basis. In itself, this wasn't a problem, except that the way we were organised meant that we still had to do routine visits to other families and facilitate plans when the worker wasn't on duty, according to the diary. For qualified workers this meant less time to deal with the extra paperwork, meetings and commitments that child protection work entails. The work that was referred to us continued to be of the complex and time-consuming variety, so that, whilst still holding about half the number of cases which social workers on other teams held, what with all the other responsibilities, these changes bit hard.

We had previously had a visit from the newly appointed assistant director, who had told us that there were no plans for re-structuring of services, but since that day the process of serial re-structuring has continued unabated. I was still happy though because, although I was not as available to clients, I was still able to engage in good practice and to work towards de-registration. Unfortunately, since plans could not be progressed as quickly as before, the turnover of work was much slower, with children and young people languishing on the register, due to the increasing loss of co-operation of parents, amongst other things.

The qualified members of the team held 'team leader' status and the rota was arranged so that at least one of us was on duty at nights when, in principle, managers were unavailable. In practice, we all knew that they were always at the other end of the phone should we need them but, to be honest, we largely managed ourselves. On one rare occasion, I happened to be on shift with another qualified worker when we received a telephone call from school regarding one of her cases. It was 3.30p.m on a Friday afternoon when the head-teacher informed Anita that two of the children, Lily (age ten) and Jane (age eight) had been talking about watching pornographic videos with their father.

The children had been registered for neglect due to longstanding concerns from the school. They always presented as unkempt and uncared for, and had a vulnerable, sad look about them. The children's mother, aged about 35, had moderate learning difficulties and the father, aged about 57, had grown-up children by a previous relationship, but had not had contact with them for many years. Anita had always said that 'dad' gave her the creeps and, on that basis, never saw him when his wife wasn't around; there was nothing on file to indicate he may be a danger to staff.

When we arrived at the house later that evening, mum had gone out playing bingo with a friend. We spoke separately to Lily and Jane to reassure them, reinforcing safety measures which Anita had already put in place. The girls more or less said their teacher was mistaken but nevertheless appeared anxious and scared. Whilst Anita addressed issues with 'dad', who denied everything vehemently, I took the opportunity to look at his huge video collection which was organised and catalogued meticulously. I also observed 'dad's' demeanour whilst Anita was talking to him; he seemed totally oblivious to my presence and, in a peculiar way, 'captivated' by Anita. Anita is attractive, very petite and almost 'childlike' in her physical appearance. We came away from the house with very uncomfortable 'gut' feelings and I understood what Anita had said previously; watching him with Anita had made my flesh crawl.

Much later, when I was overlooking this case whilst Anita was on leave, Lily arrived at our place of work looking dreadful. She had apparently taken a detour en route to school and asked a taxi-driver to take her to social services. Lily had forgotten the way to the unit, some five miles from her home, and been to various establishments, care of the driver, asking for Anita or me, but to no avail. I paid the taxi-driver, brewed up and made toast for Lily and sat on the settee with her, giving her a cuddle. Lily was distraught and could hardly get her words out but managed to say that when Anita had been asking her how things were at home, she had lied. When asked what she meant, Lily said her father made her 'do things' and gave a graphic account of what a number of these 'things' were; she also said her father made her bring some of her young neighbours to the house when mum was out, in order for them to dance naked for him in exchange for money.

Lily later gave a very impressive video statement to the police, and her father was arrested and imprisoned on remand. The family were devastated and the children miserable and full of self-blame, especially Lily. No matter what, Lily and her sisters loved their father dearly and were confused and badly damaged by what he had done. Their father had a heart attack and died the day before he was due in court. Thankfully, for the children's sake, he had given a full statement of guilt prior to his death. Nevertheless, Anita was close to tears when she told me how, when she returned their father's belongings from prison, the children leapt upon them sniffing his clothes and crying.

Meanwhile, the team was undergoing a kind of identity crisis; expectations of other professionals, families and the 'system' remained the same, in that we were available and provided 'intensive support'. We had a good reputation with schools and foster carers, and all with whom we came into contact expected and demanded the service they were used to. We ceased to operate as the team we once were and lost track of each other's cases. As such, responses to crises became piecemeal, patchy and of a much-reduced efficacy. Frustrations arose within the team as unqualified workers would continue to try to respond to their own cases and those of colleagues as they had previously, whilst qualified members of the team were unable to reciprocate. We plodded on.

We still managed to give a good service, though I often worked more and more on my own time and it was impossible to keep up with the paperwork. I remember that, at this time, two of the unqualified staff were encouraged to undertake DipSW training on a part-time basis; this meant that more work had to be undertaken by the rest of us when these workers were not on shift and there were no reductions in case-loads. They were later seconded to study on a full-time basis, which meant that we were hardly able to run the service at all. Around this time I began to work with the Roberts boys, aged nine and ten, who were registered due to neglect and emotional abuse. I had not worked with the family for very long when it became apparent that they needed to be removed. Both boys were 'beyond the control' of their mother, who was suffering from depression and a long-standing addiction to alcohol. These boys were not attending school and had no investment whatsoever in their family, community or society at large; their 'home' looked derelict and their mother was permanently under the influence. I visited often to try to engage Ms Roberts and, in the process, to gather sufficient evidence to remove the boys.

During the period of my involvement I tried everything I could think of to try to improve the situation, working closely with other professionals who were also deeply concerned. Ms Roberts consistently refused to access the help she needed to address her own needs, blaming the children for the family's current plight. I set up counselling appointments and referral to the drugs and alcohol team, making myself available to transport Ms Roberts and support her attendance as part of the protection plan. As time passed it became clear that the children's risk-taking behaviours were increasing; they had set fire to their curtains whilst their mother lay asleep on the settee, after falling asleep in a drunken stupor. The boys were fending for themselves more and more, and were observed to have been bashing baked bean cans with sharp stones, eating the contents with their fingers. The older boy had taken to hanging out outside the drug rehab centre and, on two occasions, had returned home in a taxi with money in his pocket, and both boys had been apprehended begging and stealing food. As if this wasn't enough, they had also begun to sleep in burned-out cars or derelict buildings and their mother did not report them as missing. There were no other suitable members of the family who were able or willing to look after the boys.

This was a catastrophe waiting to happen. I had discussed the need to accommodate these boys with my manager, on many occasions; he agreed but, after each discussion, came back with senior management's decision not to. At my insistence, the case was discussed with the assistant director, who said that accommodation would not take place without a full core assessment, which is a hefty document to get through. I had neglected my other cases and had a cartload of paperwork outstanding; it was Friday and, technically, my weekend off as I'd worked the previous one.

I don't have a problem with calculated risk-taking – it goes with the job; it's a sad fact that some kids lead a sad and miserable existence but, in the main, they should remain their parents' responsibility and not the State's. However, on the basis of what I had seen with my own eyes I was very concerned and the evidence was well-documented on the case-file, along with management decisions. As the children's social worker I took my responsibilities seriously and took said documents home with me. I worked all weekend, leaving no stone unturned, in order to make a 'cast iron' case. I also felt that, given the boys' familiarity with their area, an out of area placement was needed as it was obvious that they would continue to place themselves at risk if left within the borough; this was refused. In the event, I had to stay behind for three hours after my early shift on the Monday, to complete the paperwork for the fostering department. Fortunately, there were no 'in-house' placements available, so that the next day myself and a colleague transported the boys, which meant a three-hour round trip for us, returning at 1a.m., as one of the boys absconded minutes after arrival at the placement.

I 'forgot' my eldest daughter's birthday that week and also my wedding anniversary. When it dawned on me I was mortified because, daft as it sounds, I always either visit or phone and embarrass my grown-up kids by singing 'Happy Birthday' to them. I chased around with a bunch of flowers, an apology and some money in lieu of a present and felt awful about it. Martin was much harder to placate and didn't speak to me for a couple of days. He'd bought flowers, wine and a card, and had booked the night off work especially. When I rushed home late I was too knackered to be bothered and we had an argument anyway. I'd hardly seen Adam that week either and was feeling quite guilty about everything; I tried to make it up to everyone in the weeks to come and ended up feeling like I'd gone through a hedge backwards.

In terms of the Roberts' boys, I realise that what had only taken me a couple of months to get to grips with would have taken a lot longer had I been making the 'statutory' six-weekly visits. In this case I would have been completing the paperwork gradually, relying on others to express concerns, and working reactively rather than proactively. I didn't know how to work in this way – I still don't. Moreover, I don't want to. This is the 'if you don't look, you don't see' approach, which means you don't have to do anything. As a result, it's possible to take on double the caseload, making a good job of nothing but being accountable for everything.

I make no apologies for taking my responsibilities seriously, as I firmly believe that these boys were one step away from disaster. What I do question is that if the boys had been deliberately injured by their mother they would have been immediately removed because they would have had to be. The requirement for reams of paperwork before the event I saw as a deliberate attempt to stall the inevitable and a total disregard for professional judgement. Of course, I still had to complete the necessary paperwork required to accommodate the boys and to persuade Ms Roberts that 'Voluntary Accommodation' was in the boys' best interests. I had to work double shifts for the rest of the week in order to maintain my commitments regarding the rest of my caseload. I was reminded of this case quite recently, during a training event on 'the neglected child'.

Eminent speakers addressed attendees regarding the physical and psychological impact of severe neglect, and examined the issues in depth. The old chestnuts were cited, such as lack of communication between professionals, inexperienced workers, lack of knowledge, and failure to recognise a worsening in the situation. From a legal perspective, the appalling nature of disorganised case files was highlighted, along with the social workers' lack of knowledge regarding the family. Implicit within the content of the day was a serious assault on the 'common sense' of the worker. The question of impossible caseloads, given the complexity of the work, is paid lip service, if considered at all. As far as I was concerned, the speakers were largely preaching to the converted and senior management were most notable by their absence. I couldn't contain myself and, metaphorically speaking, grabbed one of the speakers in the car park as she was leaving, whilst I was going out for a fag. She told me that she understood fully, from the days when she was a practitioner. I told her things were much worse now, since the introduction of more paperwork, government targets, performance indicators and statistics requiring proof of the good practice that there isn't the time to engage in.

Anyway, at the time, I returned to the business of playing 'catch-up', only to find a series of mishaps and complications due to the fact I'd needed to take my eye off the proverbial ball to attend to the Roberts boys. Over the next few months things didn't get any easier and there were a number of further changes.

The assistant director attended the next team meeting and announced that a committee was to be set up regarding 'family support' in order to consider 'what it is' and 'how it can best be delivered'. She wasn't impressed when I tactfully suggested that it may be helpful to have someone 'who knows' from experience to join the committee. What the findings were is anyone's guess; we were never told. It was also decided that the qualified members of the team would undertake child protection investigations on the team's cases if needed, which was previously the domain of another team. Additionally, where children had been accommodated, the case was to remain with the team as opposed to being transferred as they would normally have been. There were just three qualified workers at this time, the fourth having recently defected to the fostering department.

Whilst hindsight is a wonderful thing, I don't think it would have helped me at this particular time. I was instructed to bring the Roberts boys back into the area as soon as a place was available, due to the increased costs. I spent much of my own time compiling a report which evidenced that this was not in their best interests and enlisted the help of the consultant clinical psychologist, who also put something in writing. It didn't make any difference and I was summoned to my manager's office to be told that his manager had instructed him to 'get a grip' of me. By this time both boys were settling fairly well, attending school and had built up good relationships with their carers. Alas, things had changed little since I worked with Naomi, except that now we receive awareness training on the impact of the damage we do. Nevertheless, I remained committed to my work and had firmly ensconced myself on the inner workings of my own personal treadmill.

Funny, I wasn't singing on my way to work anymore, but I hadn't had time to notice.

Chapter 12

It's difficult to pinpoint exactly when it all began to go completely mammaries vertical. It always is when you're in the thick of it. I was aware that I was pushing myself to the limit but there didn't seem to be a way out. I recall that I was constantly thinking that if I could just catch up this week, things would be okay. I was wrong. Of the three qualified members of the team, I had already watched one of them descend into the depths of her own private hell. Helen had taken on an extremely complicated case, which was in the early stages of care proceedings, and was totally unprepared for it. Like me, she had been 'hired' as a family support social worker and, as such, had no experience in court work whatsoever. Moreover, neither the manager nor assistant manager had any more knowledge of proceedings than we did. In terms of child protection work, the three of us had more experience than management; this left us all in an extremely vulnerable position.

Changes had been slow moving over a period of time but no one had thought fit to consider that the team would need support. In fact, it was never identified as an issue. The main social work teams were in a mess and unable to respond to the volume of work which was stockpiling. As far as upper management were concerned, here were three social workers who could be used to soak up the deficit. Our own managers were really not at fault; they were as lost as we were and just plodded on. Because the expertise we needed was not available to us on the team, whenever we needed guidance and support, we were redirected to other teams by management. This met with little success as these workers were overburdened themselves and, as I later found out, they were pissed off by the fact that they were being paid social work rate and being asked to provide almost 'management support'. As a result, I was often greeted coldly and told to consult my own manager. We eventually stopped asking and began to learn mostly by trial and error, which was a long-winded and anxiety-provoking state of affairs, taking up more and more of our own time.

Around this time, the manager informed me that we would be required to complete a post-qualifying course (in line with government requirements) and that one of the three of us needed to undertake this immediately. Helen was in no fit state and Anita had refused as she was more than three months behind with her written work, which left me! I don't know what I was thinking at the time. In retrospect, I didn't have much time to think outside of work obligations and just got on with it. I think I felt that I would get quicker as I became more familiar with court procedures and report formats, and adjusted to the new role. I underestimated myself, because whichever way you look at it, there just weren't enough hours in a day. Besides, the post-qualification training was designed partly as an academic exercise for social workers to evidence competency in 'good practice' and partly to 'raise the bar', in terms of a more professional profile for social work as a whole. As such, there was nothing new to learn that couldn't be learned 'on the job' and, on my first day, I found that the first module related to discrimination. The object of the exercise was to produce written work detailing understanding of the sources and impact of discrimination, in addition to 'proof' of good practice based on cases worked with. I felt a silent scream deep within but resolved to see it as just another hurdle I needed to jump.

With hindsight, the team (myself included) were becoming increasingly more dysfunctional than the families we were dealing with, which mostly impacted upon Anita and me. My relationship with Martin was deteriorating as we spent less and less quality time together. I was not as available to my daughters and grandchildren as I wanted to be, and Adam was not getting a good deal either. By this time, my sister Bet and her husband had moved back to the village, as job opportunities dried up in the West Country. I had very little time to see her or the rest of the family, which caused me to feel selfish and miserable. I spread myself so thinly on the ground that I began to only ever be available if there was a problem; every minute I spent with my family meant another minute's sleep lost because I always had a clutch of paperwork to complete before bedtime. Of course, I still needed to support Adam, which I did to the best of my ability. Unfortunately, because of the pace at which I was careering through work and life, I began to become more and more exasperated with him when I had set time aside for a specific purpose and he wouldn't play ball.

In the middle of all this, Jess was expecting her third child and was rushed into hospital six weeks prematurely. I was worried about her as she had been unwell for a number of weeks. Over the next two weeks, I rushed about between work, hospital and Adam, hardly ever being at home except to sleep. Martin took on a great deal of transporting other family members to the hospital, as I just didn't have the time. I was at work when I received a call from Jess's husband to say that Jess was in labour. The midwife allowed me to help in her delivery and beautiful baby Alicia graced us with her presence some hours later. I left the hospital with mixed feelings; I was elated, relieved, exhausted and overwhelmed. I also realised that I had lost a number of hours working time, which I desperately needed to catch up on, and I worked very late into the night, stopping for only an hour or so to return to the hospital. Alicia remained in hospital for a few weeks following her mother's discharge; when she came home, I took leave from work to support Jess. Alicia was a calm and contented baby generally, but Jess was exhausted and Alicia had taken to sleeping all day and being awake at night. Me and Jess came up with a plan whereby she tried to wake her during the day for her feeds, etc., whilst I cared for her during the night. It only took a few days to get her into a manageable routine.

At the same time, James had begun to drink again; he started out by calling into the pub for the 'odd half', but soon worked his way back to drinking several pints a night, every night after work. This impacted heavily on Adam and the girls, who were very worried about him. Adam took the brunt of it, since he was living with his dad and had to put up with the fall-out on his father's return from the pub. When drunk, James began to tell Adam that he didn't have long to live. I was livid because, whatever issues his father had, Adam was least able to cope and had enough problems of his own. I wanted Adam to come home but, understandably, he had got used to having his own space and, for better or worse, at least had some kind of relationship with his dad after all these years. I had to tell Adam that, when drunk, his father had been saying these things since he was 23 and had spoiled Jess's 21st birthday party by telling her the same thing. It wasn't long before James began taking Adam out with him, fuelling his difficulties with alcohol. Of course, as with James, alcohol exacerbated and amplified Adam's problems and I was powerless to intervene. For a time, Adam became his father's drinking partner and I had to stand back and hope it would run its course.

I began to wish I was working at Tesco. At least I would be working full-time instead of all the time. My stress levels were rising and, although I tried to be there when my family needed me, in retrospect neither them nor me got any pleasure from our get-togethers because I was always pre-occupied with what I needed to do. Martin was always on my back because I was constantly worn out and I could never do anything at a leisurely pace. 'Me' time just wasn't a consideration and I was lucky if I had time to drag a brush through my hair. Things came to a head one Saturday night. I was sitting in bed trying to do some written work for the post-qualifying course I was enrolled on. Martin had gone out on his own for a drink, following a row because I was too busy to join him. I had spent much of the day catching up on the 'firm's' paperwork and Adam had spent the day with us. At around 10p.m. Adam came upstairs wanting to talk through some of his anxieties and was particularly agitated. I was exhausted and began to scream at him about how busy I was; mid-shriek, it dawned on me and I questioned what the fuck I was doing. I had almost accepted that my professional responsibilities had taken over my life, that I didn't even have a life, but I was sure as hell that my family had to come first when I was on my own time. Granted, I had been given one afternoon a month to attend university, but with no reduction in caseload, this meant nothing. I rang the university to inform them of my decision to withdraw from the course. A few days later the tutor rang back to ask why; I explained that my work was already taking up much of my free time and said I would return if and when it was possible to complete the course on the 'firm's' time.

Me and Martin went on holiday to Greece, but I can't say it was a pleasant experience. I spent most of my time sleeping, either in bed or at the pool, and had great difficulty in trying to relax. Apart from going out to eat, I couldn't drum up the enthusiasm to go anywhere, spending my evenings in the apartment or reading on the balcony; I just didn't feel like being sociable and 'chewing the fat' over something and nothing. I'd had to work like a dog to get stuff done at work and knew I'd have to do the same when I returned. Martin ended up going out on his own most nights; after all, he'd looked forward to the holiday all year. I was unwittingly beginning to treat my family as James had treated me, only his omissions were due to alcohol addiction whilst mine were in the name of work.

By this time, I think I'd lost my sense of humour, or at least misplaced it temporarily. In the office, we were 'hot-desking' – a concept obviously thought up by someone with absolutely no idea of the work we undertook. This meant that we were unable to call a desk our own. You'd rush out on a visit, leaving mounds of files and paperwork arranged on the desk, only to return to find someone else using the computer and your stuff unceremoniously dumped, in no particular order, elsewhere. Of course, you would also claim 'vacant possession', thus doing the same to someone else. It would take a dog's age to get yourself organised again. Additionally, due to the firm's fears regarding the 'suing culture' within which we live, staff were dispatched throughout the borough in order to demonstrate correct positioning of chair and self in order to avoid repetitive strain and other injuries. I remember half-hysterically telling her that I don't have time to go for a pee because of the workload and now that we are 'hot-desking', the chances of adjusting chairs and posture several times a day was highly unlikely. Not that it mattered to anyone – after all, we'd had the training so the council had discharged its responsibility in the event of any injury.

We had the usual round of questionnaires regarding job satisfaction and what the 'firm' could do to assist you in executing your duties. I didn't hold back and suggested a reduction in workload would be most helpful, not just on a personal level but also to stem the mass exodus of experienced social workers which was increasingly leading to the employment of agency and inexperienced workers and, ultimately, the inefficacy of the department. I knew it wouldn't make any difference because the statistics would be manipulated following collation and lost in the mêlée, if published at all.

As part of the 'staff-care policy', a free online health assessment was on offer, along with initiatives and advice on achieving a healthier lifestyle and a better work/home balance. I was incensed! I would've loved to know what the uptake was from social workers, since everyone I spoke to responded by rolling their eyes. Of course, this information was unavailable, as statistics were not broken down into employment groups, and so the initiative was pronounced a resounding success. Later, there were to be visits from council staff handing out free pedometers and water bottles, and offering pieces of fruit from a basket they carried, in order to meet the council's targets. Of course, this meant another box could be ticked and left the social work department free to continue subjecting workers to the conditions much more likely to make them ill. I tried to engage social workers from other teams to join together in challenging workloads, with little success. I can understand why, since the newly qualified were concentrating on 'learning' the job, whilst others were bailing out at the rate of knots.

Meanwhile, Helen plummeted from a size 18 to a size ten, her hair began to fall out in clumps, and she was working an average of 80 to 90 hours per week. It was clear to all and sundry that she was teetering on the edge of a breakdown; the only saving grace, if you can call it that, was the fact that she didn't have a family of her own to worry about. The team had so many conflicting functions that we were meeting ourselves coming back and we didn't have the systems in place to cope. One experienced social worker from another team as good as told me that it was our own fault because we were trying to help families to resolve problems, instead of doing the paperwork, attending the meetings and just 'managing' the case. Well, fuck me! I must've been doing it wrong all those years!

At any rate, Helen transferred to another team, as she felt unsupported by management. She is still putting in more hours than the factory cat in order to provide a decent service and work remains her life. The assistant manager had a stroke and subsequently took another position, whilst the manager appeared to lose all interest in the team and looked totally dejected. I felt sorry for him; ours had been a successful, innovative team, upon which other authorities had modelled their own services. He must have been devastated as, like me, this had been his life's work.

Following Helen's departure, I was next in line for court work and was duly allocated a complex case, made worse by cultural differences and language barriers; I struggled to find a co-worker to translate and advise on cultural aspects. In the event, her involvement needed to be minimal as she attended the same mosque as the family and was experiencing harassment due to the family's standing in the community. This meant more work for me and very little support from anywhere; I didn't even have access to the format for court reports and could never get hold of anyone to help.

Much worse, the court-appointed *Guardian ad litem* (as they were then known) seemed to delight in tripping me up and generally treating me like a twat. She and the child's solicitor were best buddies and completely dismissed anything I had to say. In fact, I was almost invisible. For example, the family attempted to discredit the child by claiming that she had something wrong with her brain. The Guardian and solicitor appeared to partially buy into this viewpoint, claiming that the child was not very bright, which was not so. In the court waiting-room, the two of them would sit huddled together like co-conspirators, discussing historical events and situations that caused them confusion. Often I had the answers but, since they didn't ask and mostly ignored me, I didn't tell them.

Over a period of time Olivia had come to trust me because I had spent time with her, and knew of the complexities of her circumstances and fears regarding the future. Olivia was born in England and, unlike her family, was quite westernised in terms of her identity and had little interest in her family's country of origin. Olivia would pretend she did not understand the Guardian or solicitor's questions, if she felt it was a contentious issue that may have implications for her future. Having had long-standing involvement with the family, I knew that Olivia feared being returned to her family and that anything she said, at this stage, would be used against her should this happen.

After all, we had first become involved with the family when Olivia had disclosed to her teacher that she had awoken in the early hours one morning to find her sister's husband masturbating over her and that he had 'wet' her nightclothes as a result. Olivia's father's solution to the department's concerns was to take his son-in-law's side and to send Olivia to her room whenever he visited. Consequently, Olivia was guarded in her dealings with adults and carefully considered what she said and to whom. She also told me that she didn't get on with the Guardian and solicitor because they talked to her as if she was stupid. The Guardian dismissed me when I tried to explain and the fact that Olivia was unable to identify the geographical location of the family's origin on a map seemed to add weight to the assumption that Olivia didn't understand. Quite the reverse, Olivia was extremely bright, as her school records showed, if anyone had been interested enough to consider them.

I placed Olivia with an extended family member on the outskirts of London, which made it difficult for me to do statutory visits. I was meeting myself coming back and no matter how many hours I worked, I couldn't catch up. Because of the chaotic nature of the cases I was dealing with, one or another would require my attention, meaning that paperwork would continue to pile up. I had to visit Olivia to speak to her carer, which meant meeting up with an interpreter at the railway station in London. It turned out to be a 15-hour round trip, which was exhausting, but I was given the next day off. Unfortunately, I had far too much work to catch up on to take it.

I had been informed that the department wouldn't fund airfares – even though it would have halved my working day – because 'it wouldn't look good' and may be perceived as a waste of resources. I felt so angry when I later discovered that it would actually have been cheaper to fly, given that I'd had to take three trains. Moreover, at court, I'd overheard the Guardian and solicitor talking of their joint visit to Olivia, staying overnight and travelling back the next day; funded by the firm no doubt! I was pissed off. They had even managed to 'do lunch' together, after a shopping trip in the city centre. Following another heated altercation with the Guardian, again over something she refused to listen to, I rang the borough solicitor for advice. He stressed I needed to get on the right side of her; he just didn't get it, so I repeated what she'd said about him. Her exact words were, 'There's nothing worse than the combination of a social worker without court experience and an incompetent solicitor'. To which he replied, 'I'll punch her fucking lights out'. It was all downhill from there.

By this time, Katy had settled nearby with her partner and was preparing for the birth of her first (and she insists only) child. Jess was incredibly excited as, although she had three children herself, she was to be an 'Auntie' for the first time. Katy went into labour at midnight and we sat with her for the next 12 hours. When the time came, the midwife allowed me and Jess to deliver the baby ourselves, which was an incredible experience. Baby Ria arrived to the strains of 'No Woman, No Cry' (chosen by Katy to be played at Paul's funeral seven years earlier), which was playing on the radio at the time. We like to think that this was Paul's way of making his presence known, especially as she was the same weight and had been born at exactly the same time. Ria's birth also seemed to have broken the 'spell' of untimely deaths at seven-yearly intervals; she was also given the middle name of 'Scarlet', in honour of her Uncle Paul. Thankfully, it happened on my day off so I got the chance to sleep before going into work the next day.

I was approaching my fiftieth birthday but, to be honest, celebrations were the furthest thing from my mind. Two of the young people on my caseload had to be Accommodated as both had attempted suicide, due to their respective situations at home. Of course, this required completion of a clutch of paperwork but, more importantly, they needed me to help settle them in different private residential homes, due to the lack of foster carers. This took time and, although I was aware that other social workers would have completed the paperwork, arranged transport for the young people and ran, I couldn't do this. I spent time with both of them, giving whatever reassurances I could, taking the paperwork home and returning with it the next day. As far as I was concerned, this was the least they could expect from their social worker. In fact, I would never have considered doing it any other way. Of course, I knew that my 'good practice' had a price and that it was at my expense. At a conservative estimate, I figure I'm still owed pay for around 600 hours over and above those I was contracted and paid for. I'll never get it, of course. I tried to raise these issues on training events but, obviously, the facilitators didn't want to know; they too are social workers who have bailed out and now concentrate on delivering training, seemingly oblivious to their previous incarnation or to the reality of burgeoning caseloads. They're just doing their jobs and have their own 'performance indicators' to meet and evidence.

Needless to say, I couldn't keep this up much longer and began to feel quite ill. I wrote a letter to the manager outlining how I was feeling, but not before I reduced my hours to 25, stupidly giving me more of my own (unpaid) time to use to catch up with the work. I clearly stated that I was suffering from the physical and psychological symptoms of work-related stress and that I needed something to be done about it. Some of my cases were transferred but, alas, it was too late; I ended up with four months off work. I had got myself into a terrible state and was angry with both myself and the department. I blamed myself for not writing the letter sooner, because I knew full well that 'stress' was not the greatest ailment for a social worker to have on her record and there was no way the department was likely to take any responsibility for it. I received a letter from some faceless wonder congratulating me on having three years without sick leave, at the point at which I was feeling the worst.

My recovery was slow and painful. I lost confidence in myself and my ability. I spent my time trying to relax, getting my diet back on track and generally looking after myself. I also spent lots of time with Adam, which was beneficial for both of us. I got to see the girls and my grandchildren more often, which put a smile back on my face. Martin didn't want me to return, nor did my sisters or my children, all of whom had agonised and fretted over me. Nevertheless, I wasn't going to give up that easily and felt that the next stage of recovery could only take place when I returned to work. In my absence, the other two unqualified members of the team were packed off to university (even though one of them would be 60 when she qualified), having been informed that they would be unable to continue working on the team unless qualified.

On my first day back the assistant director came to the team meeting, ostensibly to conduct a 'review of the service'. She announced that, what with the four members of staff undertaking social work training, the team had effectively disbanded itself and that we were to be dispersed amongst the social work teams in the main offices four miles away. I was devastated; I think I'd clung to the idea that things would change and I had resolved never to let myself get into a mess again. This was a whole different kettle of fish and one I wasn't sure I wanted to be part of. It was such a shock on my first day back.

At the same time, I was required to attend an appointment with occupational health, where I was asked if I wanted counselling. I asked, 'What for?', and was told, 'Dunno'. The manager applied for early retirement.

On the instructions of the assistant director, non-'child protection' cases were to be wound down and closed as soon as possible in order to facilitate the move. I had mixed feelings regarding one or two of them, which I voiced, but was nevertheless instructed to close. Liz had long-standing historical involvement because of the risks she had exposed her children to as a result of the many men she had introduced to her family. It was known that two of her children had been sexually abused by one or two of these men, and a number of Liz's seven children had a learning disability. Liz was vulnerable, was failing to protect her children and just could not cope. I recently encountered the family, due to investigation of the latest concerns; following a review of the case, senior management concluded that the 'previous' social worker (me) had closed the case too soon.

In retrospect, it's clear that there was always a 'grand plan' to disband the team, as our original function had been gradually eroded and replaced by that of a front-line social work team. There was no doubt that the rationale for this had been fiscal in nature, but I hated the sneaky way in which it was executed, without regard to staff needs or wishes and feelings. At a subsequent meeting, me and Anita were given the choice of immediate transfer to another team or a 12 month secondment to help set up a team which would work to our original remit and keep the same name. This team was to consist of newly appointed, unqualified workers who would do the work but not case-hold. The poor sod that drew the short straw of telling us had no answers when we reframed his spiel into the more realistic expectation that we were being asked to work ourselves out of a job. (I say poor sod, but I do him a disservice, for he was paid handsomely for his services and has since been promoted, twice.) Although thoroughly deflated, we chose the latter option. It meant that we could retain our social work pay and, who knows what would happen in time?

I soon found out.

Chapter 13

I carried my enthusiasm for the work with me onto this new team; unfortunately, it received a mixed reception. With hindsight, I realise that the pre-existing management may have seen us as a threat and were protecting their own positions, having previously been pissed about by the system themselves. Managers within family support were not required, at that time, to be social work qualified and perhaps they figured we'd been brought in to take over. I don't know. For my part, I just wanted the work of my 'old' team to continue, as I'd seen what it was possible to achieve. Secretly, and perhaps not so secretly, me and Anita hoped there would be some way we could remain with the team following the 12-month secondment.

I tried to pass on my knowledge and experience for the benefit of the team; I wanted it to be successful but, although our remit was to help set up the team, we were very much kept to the sidelines. This was extremely frustrating and led to many instances whereby management were consistently engaged in reinventing the wheel. I still felt that, had me and Anita been allowed to participate fully, it wouldn't have taken the two years or so to get it off the ground. I remember clearly the time that management spent 'networking' with two similar teams from other authorities, in order to learn from the way in which their service was organised and delivered. Nothing wrong with that, except that these were the very teams which had set up services modelled on our 'old' team.

Anyway, we might've known we'd be shafted; after all, we had nothing in writing and, during that first 12 months, we agreed to do whatever was expected of us, in the interests of the new team and the Social Work Department as a whole. As such, me and Anita joined one of the area teams for three months, as they had virtually no staff and a cartload of work outstanding. Staff morale was extremely low and workers were fast disappearing under the deluge of impossible caseloads. Although not case-holding (thank God), we worked hard to help to mop up the mess caused by around 120 unallocated cases and delayed assessments. We also covered the duty desk. On our first week, me and Anita worked until midnight and 10p.m. on two successive nights.

At 4.30pm on the third day, it became clear that we were to be asked to stay late, due to another crisis, and there was no one else available. I had no idea that the assistant director was standing behind me when I groaned. I'd promised Adam to take him to play snooker that evening and it had taken all week to build him up to it. I told the manager that I had family commitments that night and was appalled to hear the scathing tone of voice belonging to the assistant director, saying that my family would have to get in the queue along with the rest – meaning the families we were working with. Of course, I couldn't expect her to know how committed to my work I was, or how much time I was owed but could never recover. She didn't know me. Nevertheless, I wanted to punch her and wondered which part of the staff-care policy was guiding her practice. Again I told myself I would continue to work hard, but not routinely on my own time.

At the time, there was only one team which was relatively stable; the rest were running on agency workers, inexperienced staff, and a wing and a prayer. Anyone who had any experience was either caught up in frantically trying to maintain some organisation regarding their own cases and/or trying to get out – they still are. Working conditions were a nightmare, and laughable, if you didn't have to contend with them. Staff parking was limited to the upper deck of a multi-storey building, as the council were keen to maintain revenue from the public for the more accessible car parks. As teams were located anywhere up to the fifth floor, getting anywhere in haste was impossible. By the time you got out of the building and negotiated the shopping centre, through which you had to pass to access the lift to the car park, it would add 15 minutes to the journey. Mind you, I suppose this was better than the previously trialled idea of some bright spark who decided workers could use parking facilities just outside the town centre, as it only took ten minutes to walk. Therefore, with travel time, a one-hour visit would take anything from two to three hours to complete. Around the same time, workers were asked not to make unnecessary phone calls or visits due to the cost. Funny, I didn't know anyone who had the time to do anything 'unnecessarily'.

There were no support systems in place, at least none that I could identify. Knowledge of workers' whereabouts was a hit-or-miss affair and, should anything untoward have happened, it could've been days before anyone realised. Due to the lack of experienced staff, managers were often in court and unavailable to the team. I remember completing an initial assessment on a newborn baby, following referral from the hospital. The family were hostile and aggressive, having had long-standing historical involvement with the department in a child protection capacity, and refused any support. The child's mother, Sara, was aged 15 and had a severe learning disability; maternal gran insisted that she provided care for her grandchild and supervised her daughter at all times. Checks on gran's youngest child, age seven, revealed no concerns and the health visitor assured me that she was confident in gran's ability. At the same time, gran was on the phone daily ranting and raving about being persecuted, or pitching up at the office, where I had to sit and try to reason with her, separated by a screen due to her unreasonable manner.

Under the circumstances, there was little to be done other than reinforce gran's responsibilities, ask the health visitor to keep a watchful eye, and close the case. The manager agreed. Two weeks later the child was admitted to hospital with a number of serious injuries caused by Sara's rough handling. It was subsequently discovered that Sara's brother was the child's father. There was no-one around to discuss the case with, and I was left feeling totally unsupported and wondering if I could've/should've done things differently. I later heard rumours that senior management felt that the case was closed 'too soon', an excellent cop-out if ever I heard one, and I wondered who would've taken the blame if the child had died. No prizes for guessing.

Some of the more experienced social workers kept photocopies of management decision sheets, especially those relating to decisions they didn't agree with and which seemed 'dodgy', in case they should 'disappear' from the file at a later date. Unfortunately, due to the complexity of cases, it wouldn't have made any difference because it could always be argued that the worker hadn't outlined the full facts of the case. Similarly, as most decisions are verbal, due to time constraints, it would be very difficult to prove the discussion had taken place at all. This leaves workers in a very vulnerable situation; as with doctors or any other kind of professional, should anything happen – particularly the death of a child – licence to practice is likely to be withdrawn. The Social Care Register, which is a relatively new requirement for social workers, states clearly that the worker themselves must be responsible and accountable for their own practice. At the same time, the system and volume of work discourages challenging decisions and encourages unacceptable risk-taking which it would be very difficult to justify.

I was just glad I wasn't actually case-holding. When I looked around the office there were few familiar faces; at one time I'd known everyone. The department introduced £1,000 annual 'bonuses' as part of their retention strategy. It hasn't worked. Workers were taking annual leave and spending it catching up on essential paperwork. I was continually taking calls from families, foster carers and other professionals, and making excuses for why the worker had not contacted them for weeks, knowing full well that the worker in question could only deal with today's emergency and that tomorrow would be the same. Others were producing shoddy work as a result of protecting themselves, inexperience and/or lack of support, and doing themselves and their clients a disservice. Managers, like their workers, were left to manage the unmanageable. No one seemed to care. I spoke to many other workers and their managers, some of whom were heading for burnout. I heard many excuses for not standing up for their rights to exercise professional judgement, hold a manageable caseload, and practice 'good enough' social work; some were good and some not so good. Some wanted the child protection experience before moving on; others were content to 'muddle along' the best way they could, neither rocking the boat nor thinking out of the box.

There were also a large number who'd forgotten, changed or had never really encompassed the basis of good practice but could talk the talk when required. Unfortunately, these are the ones who are ambitious and invariably end up in management positions (if not already managers), where they seem content to 'turn a blind eye' to what goes on and are not averse to lying, cheating and manipulating in order to retain their position. I was glad when the 12 weeks were up and I could return to my seconded position.

I was recalled to this team for a further three weeks later in the year. By this time, Anita was on long-term sick leave due to health problems. At the same time, the manager of the one seemingly stable team expressed an interest in me joining the team as the 'duty' worker and, having spoken to me, consulted with her manager, Gill, who had different ideas; understandably, she wanted me to join one of the ailing teams. I began to realise that if I didn't find my own job, either within or outside the department, I would continue to be used as a stop-gap at senior management's will. I was taken by surprise when a colleague asked me why I'd changed my mind about joining the team. Her manager had been informed by Gill that I was no longer interested and the position had been filled. I was furious that Gill could tell such blatant lies; I'd never done her any harm and she knew I was a good worker. When the 'duty' social worker position became vacant on another team, Gill told me I would have to interview for it. Unbeknown to me at the time, I could've insisted since I was already employed as a social worker. The truth is that Gill was busy 'empire building' and had already decided where I was going.

Having been told the 'duty' job was a 'specialist' post, hence the need to interview, I was expecting that a more advanced type of knowledge/experience would need to be demonstrated. The interview was a total disaster, since I'd had little time to prepare, because, for me, the work always came first and I had already provided a detailed account of my experience on the application form I'd been obliged to submit. It wouldn't have helped me anyway, because the questions were pitched so low that I hadn't a clue what they were getting at. One of the first was aimed at identifying disadvantaged groups within society; I could feel that silent scream developing again.

I blew it within the first two minutes by reeling off 'single parents; people with mental health problems; people with a disability', etc, etc, following it up with telling the interviewers that I felt like I was on the Generation Game. In fact, I remember I had to keep pushing 'cuddly toy' to the back of my mind.

Another question asked of me was to give an account of what I'd learned since qualifying. A mammoth task! Anyway, suffice to say I made a complete balls of it and the position was offered to a student, who was obviously able to answer the questions much better as she had less experience to draw on. I was well fucked off, I can tell you. Much later, I derived extreme pleasure from turning Gill down when she offered me the 'duty' post on a recently reconstituted team without the need to interview.

I have no illusions; they were desperate at the time and there was more work than one body could do. The vision of Gill, mouth agape and jaw dropped, will probably remain with me for some time. She had a face like a busted clog. It felt great to be in control for once and there has to come a time when principles are more important than pay packet. The icing on the cake, for me, came when Gill herself failed to secure a promotion, even though she had worked like a dog for the department. She left to work for another Authority and I hope she learned a valuable lesson; namely, those who shaft others shall themselves be shafted – eventually. I like to think of this as the 11th Commandment. At any rate, not 18 months later it has now been decided that this 'duty' role will be undertaken on a rota basis, with workers continuing to hold the same number of cases, including court work. A lucky escape for me; the remainder of the experienced workers on these teams are already looking for alternative employment. Those of us who have been around for some time know fair well that this is unworkable and that other Authorities, who have trialled it, have found it to be a complete disaster and have returned to the previous duty system.

Anyway, other than the fact that I had no idea what I would be doing at the end of my secondment, I was happy to be able to 'clock off' and go home at the end of my working day. I had kept in touch with Anita and we had often discussed the future; we both knew by then that the options were limited to returning to whatever social work team was deemed appropriate, or to remain doing the work we loved and losing 170 quid a week, being paid at the 'unqualified' rate. Anita was adamant she wouldn't do the latter, whilst I wavered between the two. I had already worked out that, given the extra hours needed to do a half-decent job as a social worker, when broken down I wasn't actually losing anything. At any rate, money has never been my 'God'. The loss of 'status', for want of a better word, was a bit harder to swallow. After all, I had struggled for years to qualify and being a 'good' social worker was all I ever really wanted. I decided I would leave my fate in the lap of the gods, for the time being anyway.

At the risk of sounding facetious and despite my initial reservations, management seemed to be learning fast. I had long been aware that a social work qualification doesn't guarantee anything – it's the experience and commitment that counts. The ethos and values of the team were in sync with mine and this was down to management. In particular, managers were aware of workers' strengths and weaknesses, and were readily available to support them. Workers were valued and treated with genuine respect. On one of the social work teams I'd worked on, the manager used to click her fingers and gesticulate in order to call you over; probably because of the phenomenal staff turnover rate, workloads and stress. Mind you, having never experienced the cut and thrust of social work teams directly, there was a certain naïveté amongst family support managers; in combination with the necessary deference to their qualified colleagues, this automatically dictates who calls the shots. Despite the illusion of democracy, it's all smoke and mirrors really.

Looking round the department at that time, nearly all the management and senior management positions were held by women. I'm tempted to celebrate this fact as testimony to the benefits of equal opportunities, the breaking down of outmoded concepts and ideology relating to women, and a subsequent increase in self-confidence. However, on the basis of my own observations, these women appear mainly to be of a certain age and/or unfettered by caring responsibilities. For many of these women, work appears to be the main thrust of their lives. The bald truth, I suspect, is that they are driven by the need to prove themselves in a 'man's' world in ways that a man would be unwilling to undertake. This sets a precedent, in terms of front-line workers, and encourages a culture in which working relationships are less than respectful. Managers and senior managers who routinely work outside hours in order to shore up the system are unlikely to have any sympathy for workers who do not wish, or are unable, to do the same.

Anyhow, I was working with a 14-year-old boy and his mother at this time, under the most impossible of circumstances. Josh had complex psychological problems which placed himself, his young sister and his mother in danger from his actions. Josh seemed unable to contain his emotions and, when angry, would try to harm those he loved; his ambivalent feelings also led to

Josh attempting self-harm as a result of self-loathing at having tried to hurt his family. There were no externally identifiable triggers to Josh's behaviours and therefore no means of reducing the risk. From the outset, it became increasingly clear to me that, no matter how intensive a support package we put in place, I was essentially wasting my time.

As usual, no-one seemed to want to take responsibility for the situation due to resource implications, even though it was clear that Josh needed to live elsewhere in order to protect all concerned. After many months, five two-hour meetings and escalating concerns that a disaster was imminent, it was agreed that Josh should be accommodated in an out of area placement, to prevent him from running off and returning home. In such situations, it is customary for Social Services, Education and Adolescent Mental Health Services to share the cost; however, Education were dragging their feet and claiming that Josh had access to part-time facilities locally and therefore they were unwilling to pay, despite the fact that Josh refused to leave the house and needed the structure of an 'alternative' education plan to meet his needs and keep him safe. This slowed down progress considerably, as Social Services were not about to fund two-thirds of the cost.

Explaining this to Josh's mother was a nightmare, especially since, although each department controls their own budget, funds ultimately come out of the same council 'pot'. The net result was stalemate, whilst Josh's case-holding social worker (thankfully not me) battled on a daily basis with her own department, compiling endless reports from home to evidence the need to either force the Education Department's hand or fund it themselves. I helped her out where I could as she was less experienced than me and, as head of a one-parent family, her own children were suffering. She didn't stay around for long.

Eventually, a meeting was organised to plan for the move as Josh was unlikely to go voluntarily. Given that the most important factor was the need to preserve Josh's relationship with his mother, the social work manager's solution was a stroke of genius; she suggested mum tell him they're going shopping by taxi and then travel the 30 or so miles to his placement, rather than more costly alternatives. Obviously, she hadn't considered either the short-or long-term consequences for Josh of having been lied to by his mother, or the damage this would cause to an already very disturbed young man. It was embarrassing to look round the room and see other professionals gawping in disbelief; still, I believe she's great at managing budgets.

In the meantime, things were much easier at home. I was able to spend quality time with Martin, the girls and Adam. I saw my sisters frequently and my grandchildren stayed over on a regular basis; in other words, I began to live a 'normal' life. We were still experiencing difficulties with the Adult Mental Health Team, as it seemed to be impossible to access anxiety management for Adam, who remained reluctant to go out. It was a terrible strain to try to prevent further erosion of Adam's self-confidence and we had been promised the anxiety management for the past three years now. It never got off the ground, either due to changes in worker, cancellation of the course, or lack of funds. He had attended one such group but unfortunately the group weren't supervised as they should have been.

One of the members, a young girl of around 20, had been talking to Adam on this first session and had told him she intended to cut her wrists. Adam had said nothing but appeared quite agitated when I collected him. It wasn't until the following week that Adam told me, by which time the girl had carried out her expressed intentions. The girl recovered but Adam told me he had enough problems of his own without hearing those of others. The facilitators were sympathetic and a referral was made for Adam to complete the course on an individual basis. It never came to fruition.

Much later, Adam was given the opportunity to attend another group which, at the time, he was keen to do. It was a bit of an organisational nightmare for me as I had to take lieu time from work to pick him up from home and transport him to and fro, making up the two hours at the end of my shifts. Nevertheless, Adam seemed to enjoy the first two sessions and I became more optimistic. We arrived for the third session to find a note pinned to the door to say the session had been cancelled at short notice due to staff sickness. The fourth session was cancelled in advance due to other priorities and, ultimately, the course was cancelled because of low uptake – which wasn't surprising. Shortly afterwards, Adam received a letter inviting him for another assessment of suitability to attend individual sessions, as the original assessment was out of date. He declined.

At work, I found it difficult not to be able to make decisions on my own caseload. In principle, in my 'unqualified' role, I was relying on referring social workers to direct the work – which really stuck in my craw. In reality, much of my work continued unfettered by outside interference. Once families were referred to the team, usually by the duty social worker, the cases were rarely allocated and were responded to by social workers who were usually totally unfamiliar with the complexities of the case and would go along with whatever plans I came up with. I still felt that the department would be 'getting me on the cheap' if I stayed with the team but, that aside, I enjoyed the freedom of being able to get on with the work.

After saying this, my work with Jodie (aged 13) and her mother was severely hampered by the fact that there was an allocated social worker. Jodie's name was on the Child Protection Register, following a brutal assault on her by her mother when drunk. Sylvia's lifestyle was chaotic, due to her alcohol addiction; she became totally unreasonable when under the influence, which confused the hell out of her daughter. I worked with Sylvia and Jodie separately, and reached the point where further progress was impossible whilst Jodie continued to stay with her aunt, where she had been placed following the assault. All parties, including Jodie, were in agreement with a planned return home; the social worker was dragging her feet and my manager would not allow me to continue with my own plan, since it was the social worker's responsibility, which I kind of understood. It took weeks and the family eventually made the decision themselves, which made my job harder. At the Child Protection Conference, the social worker lied to cover her own back and made the family look really bad, when in fact it was her fault. I did feel sorry for her though; she was snowed under, had little experience and was adamant she wouldn't work on her own time. These are the choices we make.

And then along came Natalie. Natalie was 14 when I first met her and in a mess; she was in self-destruct mode and was referred to the team due to imminent family breakdown and associated fears that she would need to be taken into care. During the time I worked with Natalie, the case was never allocated to a named social worker and, due to the complexities of her circumstances, I knew it was useless to discuss anything with the team's duty worker as this function was executed on a rota basis. Anyway, I knew from experience that she would have bigger fish to fry.

Intellectually, Natalie was far in advance of her chronological age; emotionally, she was still 14 and had experienced things that no one her age should have to. Natalie had struggled for a number of years to negotiate her way through life, hampered by impossible circumstances and family relationships. Her parents had their own difficulties, which impacted heavily on Natalie and were screwing her up big style. Without going into the heartbreaking details, I can safely say that Natalie's issues were not of her own making. At the time, Natalie was not attending school, was consuming a large amount of alcohol and had been doing so since around the age of 11; she had also been self-harming for a number of years and had lacerations on her arms, thighs and stomach. Natalie's parents saw her as the problem; their own issues overshadowed everything else. Nevertheless, it was clear that Natalie loved her parents and they loved her also. This was a tricky piece of work, since Natalie was, understandably, initially resistant to adult 'guidance'; after all, it had never done her any good in the past.

It soon became clear that any attempt to discuss Natalie's emotional needs with her parents would worsen her situation at home. Besides, there was very little that could be done to persuade her parents to make the necessary lifestyle changes to support her. In fact, these issues were shrouded in secrecy and not for public consumption. Frustrated that I couldn't address the underlying problems, I had to content myself with trying to build a relationship with Natalie and to convince her, somehow, that there was another way.

There were numerous crises along the way and Natalie's home life continued to be far from stable but, gradually, she was able to work through her difficulties. Natalie eventually came to terms with the fact that she would never change her parents or her current circumstances, but that she could deal with it differently. Thank God she had the maturity to do so. Natalie returned to school and, despite being pregnant at the time, she completed her exams and has remained alcohol free. She has never self-harmed since I first met her. I remain in contact with Natalie; she is 17 now and has a beautiful baby boy. Natalie has completed her first year on a Social Care course and is set for university. I am amazed at her strength of character and ability to overcome her difficulties; she is an incredibly resourceful young lady and I am very proud of her.

Every now and again someone comes along to remind you why you chose to do the job you do. Natalie is one of these people.

Chapter 14

As my secondment came to an end, I was in turmoil. I eventually decided to return to the 'social work fold' and was told I would be joining another area team in the New Year. I knew this team was the worst of all at the time; staff were just not staying, caseloads were high and there were few experienced workers. My family, including Martin and the girls, begged me not to go back. I understood why. The problem with being committed to your work is that you don't know how to engage in bad practice. It's not that I'm 'soft' and I may be old-fashioned but I wanted to actually know the names of the children on my caseload. I was unhappy with the decision from the off but thought I would give it a try. In the event, I was recalled the week before Christmas out of desperation.

I was greeted by the manager, who welcomed me with open arms. In that first week, I got stuck into the backlog of referrals and unallocated cases and did the best I could. I found out that, on her return from sick leave, Anita would be joining us and this made me feel a little easier. Again, management support was most noticeable by its absence, as both manager and assistant were in court most of the time. I managed to catch up with the Roberts boys' current social worker but unfortunately there wasn't much good news. The boys remained in the care of the Local Authority and their mother remained permanently under the influence. Due to the number and complexity of cases which the social worker carried, he had been unable to support the mother in maintaining contact with her sons. The older boy was beginning to worry about his mother as a result of not seeing her; well, to be fair, he had always had anxieties about his mum and, despite the neglect, they loved and needed each other. Regular contact with his mum was what had maintained him in his foster placement and he had eventually run away to be near her. He was now apparently totally out of control and on self-destruct. I felt sorry for them and for the social worker who felt responsible. He was in the middle of an investigation into the death of a baby on his caseload and he looked terrible. He left shortly afterwards.

I also spoke with the assistant team manager, one of the few I had known for some time and who was still around. She told me she was hanging on for her pension! She was only about 50 so had some time to go. I did understand, but I suppose because mine isn't worth much and I'm only entitled to a small portion of the state pension, I guess it doesn't really affect me. I also knew, from my own experience, that certainty in life is largely illusory. I told her that the graveyards are full of social workers just hanging on for their pensions. Interestingly, no-one ever seemed to think that there was another way – besides leaving. It never ceases to amaze me that a group of people who ostensibly spend their life working with the most vulnerable and oppressed people are afraid of standing up for themselves.

I finished work for the Christmas period with very mixed feelings. Although I'd worked hard this week and enjoyed it, I knew full well that I'd be case-holding in the New Year. The two agency workers who had sat opposite me had confided that they were looking to leave. I knew this would cause extra pressure as it would probably take weeks to fill the post, even with other agency workers. I had a crap Christmas; I couldn't settle sufficiently to enjoy the company of my family or the time off. I remember sitting for hours trying to weigh up the pros and cons of staying with the team I'd helped set up. It was Boxing Day 2004. I sat by the T.V. watching the devastation of the Asian Tsunami. I thought about the turmoil that the survivors must be going through; the loss of loved ones, homes, possessions and hopes for the future. I also thought about the trials and tribulations of my own life, what is really important in life and again wondered what the fuck was wrong with me. At the end of the day, no matter how committed I was, it's a job and shouldn't dictate my life or define me as a person. I found I still couldn't let go without giving it a try. I didn't know it at the time, but my career as a social worker was in its death throes.

I arrived at my new place of work after the holidays to find that the manager was in court all day. Lacking in any other direction, I got on with trying to sort out the mangled backlog of unallocated cases. Some of the files looked like an explosion in a mattress factory, with bits of paper sticking out and no overall organisation. At the end of the working day the manager returned and called me into her office. She told me that she was

208

due to retire at the end of the next week, was in court for the next two days and then on leave so that, basically, this would be the last day I saw her.

My heart sank as she reached for a dozen or so files and proceeded to go through each, saying, "This is in court Monday; this one Wednesday; this is in a mess and needs some urgent attention; you'll have to take this from Jim because he's heading for burnout"; etc, etc. She followed it up by telling me that, had she been staying around, she would've supported me and brought me up to date with the cases but, as things were, she couldn't say what would happen; she advised me to spend the weekend trying to familiarise myself with the cases. I was devastated. These were complex cases. I had little court experience and didn't have a clue where anything was up to. I had also promised myself that I would not, routinely, work on my own time; I'd seen where that got me the last time. The manager also said she was formally allocating these cases to me as of today, wished me good luck and left. I was bereft.

I left the office, two hours after the official end of the working day, in tears. I understood that the manager had now completed her contractual obligations prior to retirement – by offloading everything on me. This was not how it was supposed to be and, after all, it shouldn't have been my problem. I drove home in a fog and rang the manager of the team I'd helped set up. I told her I'd changed my mind and wanted to stay with the team. When I turned in the following day I was greeted coldly. The manager was leaving for court but took time out to tell me she had been angry and disappointed on hearing my decision and that, having seen my work, she knew I was perfectly capable. I told her that, as far as I was concerned, my capability was never an issue. For me, it was whether I wanted to be working all hours God sends pushing papers around, never getting anywhere and not knowing the families I wrote about, or the actual reality of their lives. I agreed to stay until the end of the week to run the duty desk.

You'd have thought I'd be happy with my decision but it wasn't as easy as that. Although I was glad to be back doing preventative work, I rejoined the team, not as a social worker, but now as a family support worker. In the early days I was a bit of a nightmare. In a sense, I suppose I was grieving for the loss of everything I had worked for and Christ knows I was stubborn and refused to be beaten; I'd had to be in order to overcome personal obstacles and trauma. A few of the other social workers told me they thought I was 'brave', whatever that meant. I certainly didn't feel brave. I experienced all the usual emotions relating to grief and loss, including being angry with myself for feeling that way.

Management and colleagues were supportive in giving me a 'wide berth' to allow me to work through stuff in my own time. Eventually I accepted that, having been a 'good' social worker, I would now be a 'good' family support worker. The assistant team manager was brilliant, as was the manager. Of course, they understood how I felt but couldn't really do anything about it. Initially I felt resentful that, knowing the job inside out, I was to be managed by unqualified personnel and that the assistant team manager had worked on one of my cases as a family support worker. I didn't feel that way for long because I got on so well with both of them. At the end of the day, whether in a qualified or unqualified post – it made no difference. I would use my knowledge, skills and values in continuing the preventative work that I loved. The fact that I had the time, since I wasn't case-holding, was a bonus; it meant that I could get a better picture of the family and issues involved, and/or provide the social worker with the evidence s/he would need and didn't have time to get directly, in the case of management decisions which clearly weren't in the interests of the child.

I only wish it was as easy as that. Although the drawbacks of being a case-holding social worker were clear, as a support worker it can be even more difficult to make yourself heard. This was the case with Anna and her daughter Freya, aged 12. Freya had been referred to the department following concerns she had been sexually abused by the babysitter, had taken an overdose and continued to say she wanted to die. The Adolescent Mental Health Team had tried to work with mother and daughter, but Anna felt it was 'no big deal' and her daughter's self-harming behaviours were increasing. Freya was adamant she wanted to proceed to court and her mother continued to try to dissuade her on the basis that she must have encouraged him. Anna was also experiencing difficulty in managing her children's behaviours.

I spent time with Freya, who was intelligent and articulate, as was her mother. I also talked to Anna about her own history and life experiences, which she was totally frank about. It turned out that Anna had been sexually abused by her teacher, at the age of 11, just after her father had died. Anna did not hold the teacher responsible because she had enjoyed the experience and had competed with her school-friends for his attention. Anna idolised her father, did not get on with her mother and had a skewed view of relationships. Anna had later had a string of bad relationships, been an escort, a stripper, and had prostituted herself when times were hard. When Freya told me that Anna was friendly with a man believed to be a paedophile, I became concerned for the safety of the younger child, aged seven. I brought Anna back to the centre for a brew and a chat; she told me that the man in question helped her out with her son, Ryan, and that she knew of his past but believed everyone should have a second chance. Anna seemed unable/unwilling to acknowledge any potential risks and confirmed that this man sometimes took Ryan away to a caravan, unsupervised, to give her a break. Anna felt this man's presence made them like a proper family, like when her dad was alive, without the complications of a personal, sexual relationship. She described her own 'needs' as being taken care of after a few drinks at her local, with whoever she fancied and was available at the time.

There were clearly complex child protection issues here, especially since Anna didn't grasp the fact that she was the perfect target for anyone interested in her children. I arranged to take Anna to see the social work manager to further discuss the implications. The case had not been allocated and the manager reinforced concerns by telling Anna not to give unsupervised access to her children. It was acknowledged that more long term work would be needed than our 'crisis' team could provide. I spoke privately to the manager regarding Anna's need for further work in her own right in order to keep her children safe.

I later learned that a neat plan had been drawn up for a support worker to provide input on behaviour management only and the case remained unallocated. I was so frustrated because I knew it wouldn't have taken more than a few sessions to unpick things further and to support Anna in getting more specialist help. The manager in question was, at the time, co-ordinating around 120 cases classified as 'non child-protection' so, as far as she was concerned, she had discharged her responsibility. Whether it was the right course of action is debatable and I was glad I wasn't responsible for it.

At this point I decided that I wanted to write a book. The purpose was two-fold; on the one hand, I figured it would help to draw a line for me personally and reinforce the decision I had made. On the other hand, I hoped it would speak to others who were perhaps travelling the same road as me, because any attempt to challenge the status quo is unlikely to come from above. In a wider sense, I hoped it might be read by anyone remotely interested in social work training, practice and/or life in general. I was nervous. I knew how to research, review and produce academic pieces of writing but this wasn't what I wanted. I'm not knocking academic knowledge but this has to be balanced by understanding; knowledge can be acquired in a rote fashion and is guided by what others want you to know, while understanding only comes from the desire to engage with and experience what it is that you want to know. In a professional sense, such understanding is (allegedly) the bread-and-butter of social work; however, we rarely apply it to ourselves and our own positions.

I started to write notes – I ended up with hundreds of the bloody things – and had sketched out a broad framework. The trouble was that the notes I made were of the personal variety and didn't fit the structure. I also recognised my tendency to revert to a more academic style of writing, which suited neither notes nor structure and tended to obscure me, the person. This wasn't what I wanted at all. Besides, I wasn't really sure whether anyone would be particularly interested in what I wanted to say. I plodded on regardless and my 'book' became the good-naturedly standing joke in the office; a dream that no one (including me at times) thought would ever come to fruition. Even Martin told me I was wasting my time, which annoyed me greatly. I'd heard that everyone has at least one book in them and I decided that this was to be mine.

At work, it wasn't easy for me on a number of levels. I knew that to run a crisis response team we needed enthusiastic, committed and experienced family support workers as a basic requirement; we didn't get them. Those within the department didn't apply. And why should they? The pay was the same but they would be expected to work unsocial hours, according to a seven-day, six-weekly rolling shift pattern. Additionally, the pace is much quicker and the work harder. One of the problems was that senior management was adamant that this team was the same as any other family support team, in order to avoid paying anything extra such as a shift allowance or to acknowledge the expertise needed because, on paper, the social work team would be responsible for decision-making. As such, advertisements and interviews for new recruits proceeded according to the requirements for new family support workers. Unfortunately, unlike other family support teams, we didn't have the luxury of inducting slowly; it takes a number of years to get anyone up to speed and, on this team, every day you hit the ground running.

As a result, we ended up with young and very inexperienced workers and me. It frustrated the hell out of me.

I tried to support colleagues but, being a family support worker the same as them, they rarely took any notice of me, even at the very basic of levels. I understand the difficulties because management were also learning, had to stamp their own identity on the team, and needed to treat everyone the same. The net result was that, as a team, we hardly got off the ground, leaving me to wonder whether I should just stop trying. I couldn't, of course, and I also knew that it wasn't their fault that the powers-that-be consider this type of work to be 'unskilled' and that experience in areas such as youth work is a sufficient pre-requisite. At any rate, we just got on with it and, thankfully, eventually managed to attract more experienced staff who were seeking a challenge.

Speaking of challenges, one of the families we were working with at the time presented us with a number of difficulties. The parents had separated, each taking one of the children with them, and were currently involved in private proceedings regarding residency of the children. The mother had a severe bipolar disorder and we were trying to provide advice and support to her in enabling her to care for her 12-year-old daughter. The problem was that in her 'manic phase' she became totally delusional and unreasonable, which caused concerns for her daughter's welfare, as mum would refuse to take her medication. This lady was a very intelligent and attractive woman; her illness was extremely debilitating, and she suffered extreme stress and anxiety as a result of thoughts, emotions and behaviours which were out of sync with the rest of us. I can't imagine what that must be like to experience first hand. She had also developed an unrequited attraction for one of the much younger male members of the team.

Work with Angela and her daughter, Petra, was fraught with difficulties. At best we could do nothing right for Angela. In the meantime, Petra was extremely confused and often fearful of her mother. Petra was Accommodated, following a particularly distressing episode which we became aware of late one evening, when she contacted us to say her mum had locked her out. Petra was waiting for us across the road from her house. She was dishevelled, cold and frightened. Angela opened the door and invited us in, explaining that Petra was being disobedient and was refusing to tidy up after herself. At first, Angela's demeanour was reasonable and we set about trying to negotiate a truce between the two of them. It soon became apparent that this was not the case.

Angela refused any of Petra's attempts to do what she asked and Angela's requests themselves became more bizarre in nature. She appeared to seamlessly slip in and out of lucidity, becoming more and more aggressive as she went. She was wearing a long 'floaty' dress which she described as her wedding dress and began to tell us of her relationship with a high profile member of the Prime Minister's family. She was waiting for him to return for the wedding ceremony and began to regale us with the contents of her nightly telephone conversations with him. At this point me and my shift partner, Shelly, were beginning to wonder how the hell we were going to get ourselves and Petra away safely; Angela had locked the door.

Angela began to, what can only be described as roam around the room in an ethereal and theatrical fashion, pushing her face into ours, invoking spirits and inviting her daughter to join in. Petra was terrified and cowering in a corner, knowing she couldn't oppose her mum. We continued to negotiate Angela's distorted perception of reality, trying to find an angle that she would 'buy into'. We needn't have bothered, since Angela suddenly lunged in our direction, ordering us to leave and take the child with us. We didn't need asking twice and, scooping Petra along with us, catapulted ourselves out onto the street with Angela screeching demonically behind us. Shelly had peed herself amidst the furore, I think half due to hysteria and half to fear. A few days later Angela was sectioned for her own safety. Much later, she arrived at our workplace looking immaculate in a large picture hat. She had spotted Neil's car outside and had brought him a bouquet of flowers. Neil was hiding under his desk, away from the window, whilst another member of staff informed her he was unavailable. Neil was almost literally shitting himself.

By this time Anita had recovered sufficiently to return to the area social work team she was assigned to. I spoke to her pretty regularly at first and we tried to grab lunch together occasionally. It became less and less often as she became more and more pre-occupied with work. Anita is a 'good' social worker and gradually spent more and more of her own time working and trying to survive, emotionally and physically. It felt strange to be on the outside looking in and, despite Anita's protests, I saw changes in her. She wasn't happy. I tried to keep in contact with other members of what was left of my old team. I don't think any of them are particularly settled; three have already left the department, the fourth remains but not for want of trying to leave. Another has her eye on management positions, whilst the sixth has made a similar move as me.

I began to see myself in some of the social workers I encountered. Like Pat, a single parent who opted to work a four-day week so that she could be available to her children and do routine chores on a Monday. The last time I spoke to her she was working from home two days a week, in addition to the four she is contracted and paid for; she feels trapped. Others are stressed and 'snappy', miss meetings, and appear totally disorganised and incompetent. They are hardly ever available to discuss the cases they are 'holding' and we are working with which, for me, is a mixed blessing, but perhaps not so for the rest of my team. Anita told me that the latest addition to her team, a young agency worker having just completed her social work degree, had asked her advice on 'how to talk to children', as she was unsure; I can only say that the department reaps what it sows.

For me, life was becoming much more relaxed and pleasurable. Clocking off was just that and the benefits can't be overestimated. Martin confided that he'd had serious concerns over the future of our marriage and that he and the girls were always worried because I was permanently worn out. I never miss a birthday or family get-together and really appreciate the company of those closest to me. I have time to think and be me, outside of work commitments. You can't buy that sort of pleasure.

One of the relatively new permanent social workers told me that she was sticking around to gain her post-qualification training, before working for an agency at double the pay. I can't say I blamed her but it wasn't what she wanted. Jackie is extremely competent and committed, and has worked long and hard for her families and the department. Unfortunately, her relationship broke down and she discovered that her partner had been seeing someone else, no doubt whilst she was up to her eyeballs in work. I first met Jackie when she referred a single mother and her daughter to the team, on account of their volatile relationship and the mother demanding that the department take her daughter into care. Unbeknown to us, at the time, the girl had been privy to the sight of her mother's 'bits' broadcast on the internet. Her mother, Mandy, was apparently searching for partners and had posted these images for public consumption. Mandy also had a penchant for entertaining a number of men-friends in secret upstairs in her bedroom.

Mandy presented herself as a fair-minded person with reasonable expectations of her daughter. However, when seen in situ with Lara, the two of them would bawl at each other like banshees with little or no reason. Lara was staying out late, drinking and engaging in sexual activity, which her mother disapproved of; there were also difficulties with school attendance. In a funny way, Mandy came across as very moralistic and expected Lara to behave like a mini adult whilst at the same time doing as she was told, with little or no input from her. In fact, they both functioned on the same level and fought like sisters.

Individual work with Lara was undertaken, during which she spoke of her anger and confusion regarding her mother's 'secret' life. During an angry exchange at the house, Lara confronted her mother about such issues, upon which Mandy cried excessively and dramatically whilst denying it vehemently. Lara responded aggressively to being called a liar by her mother. Mandy didn't know it at the time but her ex-partner had sent copies of the internet images to Jackie, in an attempt to secure residency of Mandy's youngest child and, of course, we couldn't say we knew Lara was telling the truth.

Mandy didn't approve of make-up, which, on another occasion, had caused a row between her and Lara; we were getting used to responding to crisis calls on a daily basis by now, and to Mandy's demands we take her daughter 'into care'. By the time me and Shelley got to the house it was like World War 3. In an effort to defuse the situation I had tried to get Mandy to see that make-up is fairly normal and harmless. It was odd the way in which that statement completely changed Mandy's mood. Not wishing to be disrespectful, I have to say that Mandy was not the most attractive of young women; her eyesight was bad and she wore very strong glasses of the bifocal variety. Mandy peered out from what looked like miniature upturned jam jars, screwed up her face in her customary unattractive manner and calmly announced that she was lucky that way, in that she'd never had to wear make-up. She was calm and back in control. She might've been but I wasn't; I didn't dare look at Shelly because I knew if I got eye contact we'd laugh.

I used to wonder what had happened to Mandy to result in her contradictory and ambivalent views and behaviours. Shelly had hoped to work with Mandy to help her to consider these issues, but whatever the problem was it was deep rooted and Mandy wasn't about to let her unpick them. In the event, not much could be done due to the constant fights and arguments and so we were forced to close. This was Shelly's case and I'd never been involved other than responding to crises when on duty. Because of the volatility, I went with Shelly on her final visit, anticipating trouble. Although Mandy hadn't changed, Lara was learning to avoid her mother's wrath, to some extent, by modifying her behaviours. Things were relatively calm at the house and, on leaving, Mandy flung her arms around me and, taking me by complete surprise, kissed me full on the mouth. I stood there looking gormless, whilst Shelly stifled a guffaw. God only knows why she didn't kiss Shelly; she'd done the work, not me. We drove back to the office, me rubbing my lips raw with an old piece of tissue I found at the bottom of my bag. Shelly thought it was hilarious, as did Jackie; I'm afraid it took me a bit longer to see the funny side of it. I was used to perching on the armchair in shit-ridden houses at times and have never shied away from 'dirty jobs', but I did draw the line at being so 'up close and personal'.

Around the same time, a colleague began to work with another young girl around the age of 15 whose parents were very vocal in expressing their wish for her to be 'removed'. Sacha was unable to identify any acceptable reasons for parents to take this stance. There were the usual issues like an untidy room and failure to bring washing down which caused tension, but even these were extremely mild for a teenager. Sara was attending school but was repeatedly grounded for weeks at a time for some small, insignificant misdemeanour, the latest being for the whole of the school holidays. As far as Sacha was aware, Sara didn't smoke, drink, take drugs or display any problematic behaviours.

In fact, Sara was almost a 'model' teenager as teenagers go; attempts to reflect this back to her parents drew a blank and they wanted rid of her. Sara's existence in their household seemed to be the problem but no-one could for the life of them understand why.

I visited a couple of times with Sacha and we were amazed by the state Sara's parents wound themselves up to, over relatively nothing. They had an older son who had apparently caused them no problems whatsoever; the sun appeared to shine from each and every orifice. The mother was what I would describe as a 'cold fish' and appeared emotionally disconnected, rude and dismissive, whilst dad was vocal, aggressive and overly emotional. Mum had told us that dad had cared for Sara when she was a baby as she (mum) didn't 'take to her'. When it was found that Sara had a boyfriend (she was nearing 16 at the time) all hell broke loose. Dad's response was totally unreasonable, although he denied it had anything to do with the boyfriend.

Sacha took me with her one night, in response to a crisis call, to be told they wanted her out. We calmly explained that we weren't taking her anywhere and that the Department did not take responsibility for other people's children but were here to help. Dad went berserk; he screamed at the top of his voice that we didn't understand and weren't listening, whilst covering his head with his arms and hands. Still we could find no explanation for such depths of feeling; mum sat silently in the corner with a face like a bulldog chewing a wasp. At one point he swung out as if to hit Sacha and we were glad we were sitting near the door. We left to the tune of dad threatening to batter his daughter and then we would have to find her somewhere to go. True to his word, around a week later Sara was removed from her family for her own safety, as a result of physical abuse. Dad had kicked and punched her whilst her mother and brother aided and abetted by holding her arms during the assault. We never did get to find out what the hell was going on in that house but we did have our suspicions.

Chapter 15

We were only a small team of five workers to begin with and we struggled to cover the shifts and stay open seven days a week. Unfortunately, after the first year, only two of us remained. One transferred to another team and the other two left to take up positions as trainee social workers. I asked one of them why he had decided on this course of action. 'Money, status and power', was the reply. It made me feel sick to the pit of my stomach as I realised that this was to be the new breed of social worker. I liked Neil on a personal level, albeit he was young and very naïve; he was a 'go-getter' who is evidently set to progress quickly. Conversely, Kerry was very in tune with clients but apt to become overly involved and quickly reverted to 'rescue' mode. I thought, with experience, she would make a good social worker but advised her to stay within the voluntary organisation she is training and to avoid frontline social work. Unfortunately, this work is not suited to anyone with a conscience, a family and who wants to have a life of their own.

At this point, thankfully, we had three experienced family support workers transfer to the team and had managed to keep one of the new recruits. We had also been given the go-ahead to recruit a further three which, including me, gave us a team of eight, plus managers. This meant it was easier to run the shifts and to cover for Lisa who was about to go on maternity leave. Lisa had spent time working with a young girl, who had complex problems, and her family, who were at their wits end. 'Toni' used to talk of having had a baby and buried it in the backyard; she also spoke of her desire and intention to 'steal babies'.

One evening as we were about to finish the late shift, Toni appeared at the door with a young toddler in a pushchair. Shelly was out on a visit at the time and, although me and Lesley recognised the name and the face, we'd forgotten the details. Toni had told us she'd lost her bus fare, was babysitting the child for her boyfriend and asked for some money to get home. She acted strangely, to say the least, but the child looked well cared for and Toni was attentive to her needs. It was dark, getting late and freezing cold, so we gave her the money out of our own pocket, explaining that this was a one-off and to make sure she went straight home; Toni would've been around 17 by now. It wasn't until Shelly returned (who remembered the case well) that I began to panic, thinking Toni may have abducted the child and I'd just given her the means of escaping with her. It took a further half-hour to find the old file and ring her dad, who said she hadn't got a boyfriend, never mind one with a child. It took us another hour and five phone calls to establish that she was a neighbour's child. The three of us locked up and went home laughing through sheer relief.

At home things continued to improve, since I now had the time and energy to invest in my own family. Me and my sisters planned a weekend away, which was brilliant, and my holiday with Martin was much more relaxed this year; the petty bickering of the past was put to rest. Adam was again responding well to the extra time and attention I was able to give, and my relationships with my grandchildren became stronger and closer. Me and my daughters were able to spend more time together, subject to the combined impact of our respective commitments. To me this is what life is all about and often what is missing from the lives of families we work with.

In the case of Rhianne, aged 12 when I first encountered her, there had been no supportive adult in her life for quite some time. Unlike Natalie, Rhianne did not have the emotional maturity to cope. Rhianne's step-father had sexually abused her sister and her mother chose to keep her husband over her daughter. The department had either chosen to ignore the possibility that Rhianne may also have been abused or this had been overlooked. It isn't difficult to see how this happened but, to me, it's very difficult to justify. Either way, Rhianne had been left at home when her sister was removed. It was later discovered that Rhianne had ADHD and, during the course of the team's involvement, suffered multiple rejection from various members of her family. Understandably, the department was averse to accommodating her, since the damage had already been done, and each time we worked with Rhianne the brief was to support her placement with a variety of dysfunctional family members or friends. Rhianne quickly attached herself to the female members of the team, especially her key-worker, and maintained contact by telephone each time the case was closed. By the time Rhianne was accommodated she was 15, had been living on the streets for ten days, and was severely emotionally damaged. Rhianne was sexually active, drinking, taking drugs and was eight weeks pregnant; she was also cutting herself quite badly and had tried to take an overdose on a number of occasions.

A planning meeting was held with representatives of various other agencies and which I attended in place of her key-worker, Shelly. Backed up by Rhianne's psychiatrist, I explained that she needed a residential placement because she couldn't cope with a close personal relationship with a foster carer, due to her ambivalent feelings towards her mother, who she often tried to chase around after. Like Naomi (who I'd known from my days in residential), Rhianne used to sabotage relationships if she felt people were getting too close; she often swapped allegiances with staff on our team for the same reasons. Additionally, foster carers would have been unable to cope with Rhianne's disturbed and disruptive behaviours in their own home.

Rhianne was ultimately placed with an inexperienced carer (most certainly due to the cost), who later told me that the social worker had given little background information, save the fact that Rhianne needed some TLC. The placement broke down a short while afterwards, following Rhianne's increasingly disturbed behaviours and further incidents of self-harm. In response to a call from the carer one weekend, we removed Rhianne for her own safety due to the fact that the foster carer was continuing to argue with her whilst she was cutting herself with a razor blade. I don't blame the carer; she was totally unprepared to deal with a youngster as damaged as Rhianne.

At a later meeting, the senior social work manager was challenged, by her manager, as to why a residential placement wasn't pursued in the first place, given the complexity of issues involved. Neither me nor the psychiatrist were in attendance and so she lied, saying that the decision was made on the basis of the recommendations we had made. The social worker and other professionals who had attended the first meeting said nothing. I was furious when I found out, even though I understand her need to save face, the fact that she is responsible for the budget, and that we never have enough money in the pot. Her own manager probably knew fair well why, before she even asked the question. I rang her to say there must be some misunderstanding. At first she denied having said it, then quickly back-pedalled to say she may have but attends so many meetings she can't remember. I told her that it was okay so long as she knew it was her misunderstanding and not mine. I suppose I could have gone higher up, but what's the point? It would only have created problems for me and, in the scheme of things, it's pretty much par for the course. I was satisfied that she'd be likely to remember this incident in the future and not try it on again; fingers crossed.

I encountered a succession of 'new' social workers – mostly young and inexperienced – who were full of enthusiasm and keen to do a good job. I found myself obliged to warn them of the pitfalls of the job but tried hard not to put them off completely. Obviously they have to learn for themselves and many said they would never allow themselves to work routinely in their own time or stand for any kind of nonsense. Most have already left and the few that remain are already beginning to grumble about the extra time they are racking up and the problems this is causing. I feel sorry for them.

I began working with a 12-year-old girl at the time, whose young mum was heavily into alcohol and drugs, though she wouldn't admit it. This young girl was totally off the wall due to the absence of any appropriate guidance and supervision. She used to climb through the back window to gain access to her home and often found her mother in a stupor. Carly wasn't attending school, would often be missing from home, and would get herself to the nearest city and hang out there late at night. Carly's name was on the Child Protection Register, which doesn't afford much protection in the absence of parental co-operation – it just means there is greater pressure on the social worker and other professionals to keep track of her circumstances and act accordingly. Her mother avoided me most of the time and refused to work with me in any meaningful fashion.

Carly was a likeable kid who didn't really trust adults and just wanted to fend for herself. We used to talk about her need to keep safe, but Carly would insist she could look after herself and would 'kick them in the balls' should anyone attempt to grab her whilst out overnight. Out of desperation, I decided Carly should test this theory for herself one evening when she was with me at the centre I worked from. We'd just had a brew and a chat when she got up from the settee to leave. Taking her by surprise, I pushed her back on the settee and held her there; there was another member of staff present at the time. Carly did begin to get the message.

Anyway, as Carly's trust in me increased, she began to tell me more of the things that were happening in her life; things her mother had told her not to tell and which placed her in danger. On a joint visit with her social worker, Carly clammed up and refused to reiterate what she had already told me. In an attempt to get Carly to understand why she needed to tell her, the social worker explained that we are an 'evidence-based service' – which didn't help things at all. Eventually, I supported Carly to move in with her older sister and, whilst this was far from perfect, it was decided at a Child Protection Conference that, should she return to her mother's care, there would be cause for concern. Everyone involved with the child agreed that Carly would be exposed to unacceptable risks in this situation and that the case-holding social worker would need to consider recourse to the court in the form of a Care Order. For a number of reasons Carly was enticed back to her mother with the offer of a week's holiday in Spain. I was mortified when informed that the department were going to allow this to happen, given that everyone agreed she was not safe with her mother in this country.

I was told that the reasoning behind this was that, if there was sufficient evidence for an Emergency Protection Order to prevent her from going, questions would be asked as to why the department were not pursuing a full Care Order. I half understood this decision because, once in the court arena, all control of the case is lost and working to the often unrealistic expectations of the court is a costly and time-consuming business; time and money being two of the commodities in very short supply in this business. In the event, Carly returned home safe, although God knows what she had been exposed to and she wasn't saying. Nevertheless, I was glad I wasn't the case-holding social worker and had made my objections quite clear. I understand that Carly has recently been Accommodated and is subject to a Care Order, following her mother's continued refusal to work with the department and further incidents at home. Carly is, unfortunately, now also refusing to co-operate and appears to be in self-destruct mode.

Aside from those young people who clearly need to be 'Looked After', the team has a good success rate. Apart from the cost to the department, the benefits for families are obvious. I have to remind myself of this, on occasion, when I find myself hankering for more control over cases and perhaps feeling a little de-skilled. On balance, I feel I made the right decision, for me, and now actually have the time to go on training courses in order to maintain my registration. I still enjoy the work that I do and feel the personal rewards are enormous, since I am now very much in control of my own practice.

At the end of this second year the 'new wave' of workers are set to leave; although this time, of the eight workers on the team, we will retain four core members, including myself. The impact of the shift system and weekend working is identified as the main reason for leaving, in addition to the 'stress' of the job. It's such a shame that the investment and training is again lost and there is still so much more to learn. There is also the issue of acceptable risk-taking, which only develops over time and can seem daunting to inexperienced workers. I wonder if and when senior management will ever understand that disbanding my 'old' team was false economy, dressed up as 'Best Value'. This team had been around for some 17 years with little, if any, change in staff; the passion for the work, team cohesion, and outcomes for families meant that not a penny's investment was lost. For this, qualified and/or experienced workers are needed and their commitment rewarded. After saying this, much of senior management have 'trouble-shot', saved money and moved on, thus escaping the reality of the situation left behind.

Funnily enough, following a recent review of senior management salaries, the cumulative pay rise is around the same amount as savings made by disbanding the team and replacing it with unqualified, inexperienced workers. Another layer of senior management has been added, costing Christ knows what, and the Council continues to spend money on running stress management courses, commissioning semi-famous 'motivational life trainers' and the like, in addition to blowing its own corporate trumpet whenever the opportunity presents itself. It may be simplistic but, to me, lower caseloads and therefore the time to do the job would do the trick. At any rate, I have resolved to retain my commitment to the job during the hours I am contracted and paid for – in the interests of the families I work with. Outside of this, sad to say, the department will get what it pays for.

Driving to work the other day, I heard one of the new recruitment ads for social workers. They usually portray laid-back workers who have good relationships with service users and are able to support them through traumatic events and circumstances or to 'rescue' abused children.

I usually flick to another station to avoid opening the soap box in my brain.

EPILOGUE

My career may have come to an untimely end but I'm very much alive and kicking; which goes to show that 'you can take the girl out of social work but you can't take the social worker out of the girl.' My children are all grown up now, aged 35, 30 and 28 respectively, and I've just celebrated my 54th birthday. Me and Martin continue to live in our little 'two up, two down' cottage and life's quite sweet, comparatively speaking. Even Adam seems more settled, although still in need of the family's support in negotiating his way through life. My sisters now live in the next village and we continue to have a very close, affectionate bond. My eldest grandchild is 16 and the youngest aged five; all in all, I'm kept very busy and, as the saying goes, 'we haven't much money but we do see life'.

I continue to remain committed to my work and to be passionate about people; though I'm a bit more philosophical these days. The mass exodus of experienced social workers continues, to the point where workers have started and finished before I've even managed to remember their names; most of them continue to jump from one job to another, gathering qualifications and training as they go. There is little commitment either way and the cost of agency workers is escalating.

Call me paranoid, if you like, but I often wonder if it suits senior management to have a consistently inexperienced pool of social workers; they cost much less, don't fully understand the risks they are taking, are unlikely to challenge decisions, and can be blamed (along with their immediate managers) should anything go wrong; in combination with ridiculous workloads, this is a formula guaranteed to produce a hot-bed of frustration, bad practice and dodgy (if not dangerous) decision-making. On my own team, I hope we can find a way of attracting people with a genuine commitment to the team and the families we attempt to work with, outside the 'politics' of the game.

Within the department and, I suspect, on a national level, moves are afoot to reduce social workers' caseloads. Unfortunately, this will not involve employing more of them but will result in all but the 'heavy end' child protection and court work being case-held and managed by unqualified staff, who will become just as overburdened. The classification of 'Child in Need' and 'Child Protection' cases is arbitrary to say the least; it is subject to many influences and can change at any point in time. Many cases are labelled 'Child in Need' when statistics on child protection are high; the risks and responsibilities of unqualified staff holding these cases is self-evident. In my opinion, this will not resolve difficulties but just shunt the problem on a little to be dealt with further down the line. In addition, most managers of these staff have never been social workers themselves and are hurriedly being put through qualifying courses in order to manage those who will be case-holding.

I doubt very much whether social workers will benefit from this type of arrangement either, much less the consumers of social work services, due to the fact that all of their cases will be of the complex and time-consuming variety; colleagues who are currently relied upon to work with families to make the necessary changes are those who will be case-holding themselves and therefore unavailable. No disrespect to the many experienced support workers, but this also represents social work 'on the cheap' and a further erosion of the profession. Preventative work will become a pseudonym for preventing reception into care at all costs, rather than meeting the child's, young person's or family's needs for support and protection.

On a larger scale, the move towards increasing the academic component of the social work profession will undoubtedly produce a new breed of social worker; in the absence of life experience and the time and tools to do the job, workers will become distanced from the lives of those they seek to influence. Social work practice will increasingly become guided by policies, procedures and legislation (including the search for loopholes and associated abdication of common sense), and less by understanding of and engaging with families in attempting to resolve the difficulties with which they are faced. At the same time, pre and post-qualification training will continue to become more and more unrealistic, in terms of what it is possible to achieve on a personal level. Obviously, the cycle of incompetence will continue, with further scandals resulting in more pressure upon workers. On the basis of discussions with other social workers, there is no evidence to suggest that things are any different in other Local Authorities.

I understand that senior management are as powerless (in real terms) as their workers, due to diminishing budgets, their own performance indicators, and the need to evidence 'Best Value' and 'Continuous Improvement'. Of course, the financial and personal gains are much greater and they do not 'see' the damage being done to workers and families in any 'joined up' fashion. I am also aware of the parallels with other public sector workers, such as in the NHS, Police, Education and the Prison Service. The fact is that we do not have the resources to do the job and, whilst individuals at every level continue to mask the problems and manipulate the statistics, more and more cuts will be made alongside higher expectations and increased individual accountability. At the same time, more sophisticated and time-consuming means of evidencing accountability and professional development further restrict the time available to do the job. No one has the time to think, or if they do they ignore it, but none of us is truly taken in by the lies, damn lies and social work statistics. For my part, I grow tired of the latest management 'buzz words', such as 'thinking out of the box' and 'cascading of information'. It may surprise the upper echelons to learn that many of us have been thinking out of the box for some time and since when has information been known to 'cascade' upwards?

As I see it, the only way in which things can change is for workers to stop shoring up their immediate managers by refusing impossible workloads, forcing them in turn to admit that the job cannot be done efficiently with current staffing levels. Unfortunately, this would inevitably mean action on a national level and for social workers to stand up and be counted, in educating those in power as to what can and cannot be done. Whilst individuals continue to manage the unmanageable, the problem will remain unaddressed; workers and line managers will continue to be the scapegoats, in the event of the bad practice they are forced to engage in becoming public and the difficulty is that no-one can predict which of their complex cases will prove to be their professional nemesis.

By the way, I sing again on my way to and from work; but don't tell anyone!